1000
football
shirts

First published in the United States of America in 2014 by
Universe Publishing, a division of Rizzoli International Publications, Inc.
300 Park Avenue South, New York, NY 10010
www.rizzoliusa.com

Created by olo.éditions /www.oloeditions.com /115, rue d'Aboukir, 75002 Paris, France

Original concept /Marçais&Marchand
Editorial direction /Nicolas Marçais
Art direction /Philippe Marchand
Author /Bernard Lions
Layout /Marion Alfano
Editor /Nicolas Camus
Shirt design /Lise Bonneau, Marion Alfano
Proofreaders /Jonah Fontela, Aurélie Gaillot

Library of Congress Control Number: 2013954599
ISBN-13: 978-0-7893-2730-7

2014 2015 2016 2017 /10 9 8 7 6 5 4 3 2 1
Printed in Singapore by Tien Wah Press

Acknowledgements
olo.éditions would like to thank all of the trademark holders (clubs, national associations,
manufacturers, sponsors etc.) for the visuals reproduced in this work.
Thank you as well to Thierry Freiberg, David Ausseil and Charles-Henry Contamine for their help.
The author would like to thank Patrick Battiston, Cyprien Cini (France, RTL),
Bruno Constant (England), Garance Ferreaux (France, M6), Eric Frosio (Brazil), Stéphane Guy
(France, Canal +), Franck Le Dorze (France, L'Equipe), Bixente Lizarazu, Roque Gaston Maspoli, Jean-
Pierre Papin, Sergueï Polkhovski (Ukraine), Johnny Rep, Jean-Michel Rouet (France, L'Equipe), Alexis
Menuge (Germany), Manuel Queiros (Portugal), Florent Torchut (Argentina) and Marie Yuuki (Japan).

Preamble
In order to ensure a uniform appearance, all of the shirts have been redrawn in the most realistic manner possible.
Where a particular shirt was worn during a season spanning two calendar years, the dates used in captions refer to
the year in which the season finished (i.e. '2013' instead of '2012-2013'). The honours listed are correct as of the end
of the 2012-2013 season.
The international and continental honours only include the results achieved in the following competitions: FIFA
World Cup, FIFA Confederations Cup, Copa América, Panamerican Championship, Olympic Games, UEFA
European Football Championship, Gold Cup, African Cup of Nations, Asian Cup, FIFA Women's World Cup,
UEFA Champions League (including the former European Cup), UEFA Europa League (including the former
UEFA Cup and Inter-Cities Fairs Cup), UEFA Cup Winners' Cup, UEFA Super Cup, Intercontinental Cup, FIFA
Club World Cup, Copa Libertadores, Supercopa Libertadores, Recopa Sudamericana, Copa Sudamericana and
Copa CONMEBOL.
In the first section of the book, the order in which national teams appear is based first and foremost on their
performances at the World Cup, and then at other international tournaments.
The order in which clubs appear is based first and foremost on their performances in non-domestic tournaments.
In the second section of the book, nations are listed according to the ranking defined by the International
Federation of Football History & Statistics (IFFHS).
In the event of readers discovering any errors, they should not hesitate to write to contact@oloeditions.com so that
they can be corrected in future editions.

1000 football shirts

THE COLOURS OF THE BEAUTIFUL GAME

Bernard Lions

foreword by
Carlo Ancelotti

UNIVERSE

I was Tagnin. Dreaming of Di Stéfano.

Foreword

I was not as chubby as I am now. Back then my heart was clearly visible under a thin layer of skin. More than feel it, you could see it pounding. We're talking about the beating heart of a six-year-old child who had just been given his first football shirt. Pure emotion. Even then I was called Carletto, but that day I was not Ancelotti. I was Tagnin; defensive midfielder who, at Prater stadium in Vienna only a few months before, had taken the legendary, luminary Alfredo Di Stéfano out of the European cup final. The shirt was that of Inter, my first love, overwhelming passion and memorable better half (or rather my better third, because my size has over time become cumbersome, invading other people's space...) and the shirt that, for work, I had to leave behind.

Made from a heavy fabric, the shirt was so hot that it overwhelmed me in the winter and in the summer risked hospitalizing me for suffocation, yet it was my formula for happiness. A suit of armour against everyone and everything. Soaked to capacity during lightning storms and abominable when the sun was out. Its fibres overlapped, running, rebelling, and tangling around me. Maybe I scratched, but I kept smiling, because you cannot be allergic to beauty.

The lines were very thick, black as the fear that overwhelmed opponents, and as blue as the sky, and the secret was right there: to compose the best stories you do not need an infinite number of pages, a few lines are sufficient. Those lines. Some sweet emotions can also be written vertically. They had not yet added the numbers, nor the names to be stuck on the back, and it was all so perfect: a diamond, to be such, must remain raw. Any impurities will ruin its elegance.

That for me was *the shirt* and will remain so forever. To be used during the games of the imagination, on a field of dirt in which I saw the finely cut grass of the San Siro. Surrounded by the purest thoughts. As a player first and then as a manager, the colours would change, the boundaries also, the prospects as well, but the first love is never forgotten. Not a collector's item, simply a piece of my heart. I was Tagnin. Dreaming of Di Stéfano.

Carlo ANCELOTTI

Manager of Real Madrid, 2013–
(Former player for Parma, Roma and A.C. Milan, and
former manager of Reggiana, Parma, Juventus,
A.C. Milan, Chelsea F.C. and Paris Saint-Germain)

Contents

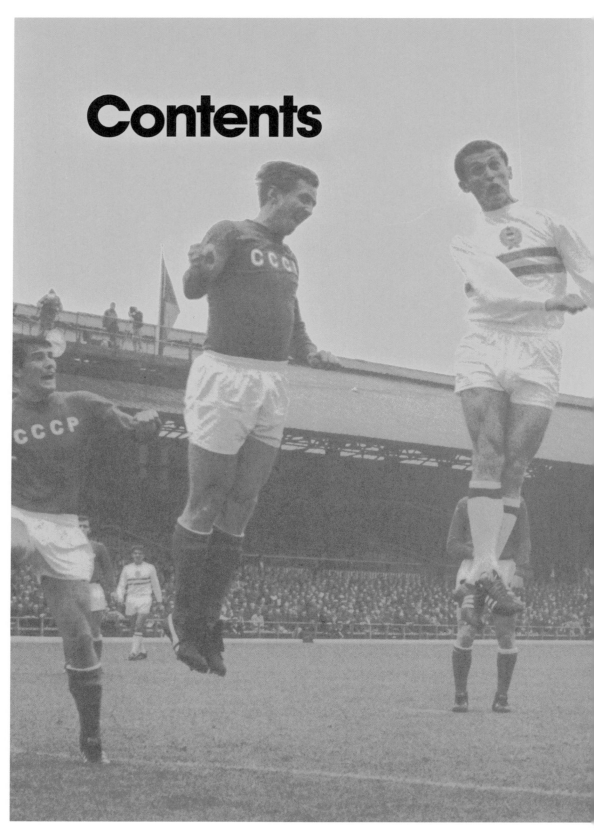

Notts County F.C., the oldest
football club in the world still
playing at a professional level.
The club was founded in 1862.
(Group photograph taken
in 1905.)

Brazil
Italy
Germany
Argentina
Uruguay
France
Spain
England
Mexico
USSR
Cameroon
Japan
Netherlands
United States

170
Legendary Shirts

Boca Juniors
FC Barcelona
Real Madrid
Ajax
Liverpool
Juventus
Internazionale
Bayern Munich
Santos
FC Porto
Manchester United
Chelsea
Borussia Dortmund
Benfica
Paris Saint-Germain

Introduction

R oger Milla couldn't help himself. When the final whistle signaled the end of Cameroon's historic win over Argentina in Italia 90's opening game, the 38-year-old Indomitable Lion chased after Maradona and asked for his jersey. With the shock of defeat still fresh, the Argentine icon offered up his stripes gladly, with a smile, draping Milla's green shirt across his own shoulders.

Some shirts remain forever connected to the great ones who wore them—Alfredo Di Stéfano in the pure white of Madrid, Maradona in the light blue of Napoli, Cruyff in his bright orange, Zidane all in royal, blazing blue. Even for the greatest players, a football jersey stirs emotions. On pitches across the world, players swap them with opponents. Sometimes after a glorious victory, sometimes in the doldrums of defeat, and sometimes even at half-time with the game still in the balance! These shirts often end up in frames, behind glass, and hanging in homes, cherished symbols of past battles.

The sight of players swapping shirts at the end of a match is now commonplace, but that was not the case until May 31, 1931. The French, delighted to have beaten the English for the first time in ten years, asked if they could keep their opponents' jerseys as a souvenir of the match. This sporting behaviour later gained worldwide acceptance when Pelé and Bobby Moore swapped shirts at the final whistle of Brazil's hard-fought 1-0 win over England on June 7, 1970 at the World Cup in Mexico. While swapping shirts at the end of a game is now customary, taking off a shirt during a game to celebrate a goal or for almost any other reason is considered unsportsmanlike behaviour and prohibited by FIFA.

Of course, there are some memorable exceptions. When Chelsea played against Reading on October 14, 2006 both goalkeeper Cech and substitute goalkeeper Cudicini left the field with injuries. Captain and central defender John Terry put on a goalkeeper's jersey and finished the game between the uprights. On April 13, 1996, Sir Alex Ferguson, down 3-0 against Southampton, made his Manchester United players switch shirts at half-time blaming the kit's grey colour for the team's poor performance. It almost worked. They got one goal back but still ended up losing the game.

Shirts do so much more than tell the history of football. They speak of legend. They stand for entire eras, stoking memories and dreams of impossible matches and unforgettable teams.

Alfredo Di Stéfano in Real Madrid's dressing room on May 25, 1956.

Brazil

FOUNDED IN THE FLAG

The World Cup immediately conjures up images of Brazil and their fabled yellow top with green trim. However, *La Seleção* has not always taken to the pitch in those colours.

The South Americans wore a white jersey from 1919 until the 1950 World Cup, which was the first to be hosted by Brazil. Although just a draw was sufficient at the time to secure their maiden world crown, Uruguay triumphed 2-1 at the Maracanã Stadium in Rio de Janeiro on July 16, 1950. The white quickly became associated with this national tragedy by the superstitious in Brazil, who were left devastated by the "Maracanaço" ("The Maracanã Blow"). *La Seleção* subsequently opted for the green and yellow of the national flag, symbolising the Amazon rainforest and the country's wealth in gold. Although the Brazilians also make use of blue, the fourth colour on the flag (including white), for their shorts and their away top, it is in the *Canarinha* shirt that they enjoyed their greatest moments of glory, lifting five World Cups.

BRASIL

9

**GLOBAL
HONOURS**
5 FIFA World Cups
4 FIFA Confederations Cups

8

**CONTINENTAL
HONOURS**
8 Copas América

2002
World Cup–winning jersey

1950
World Cup–runners-up jersey

1958
World Cup–winning jersey

1962
World Cup–winning jersey

1994
World Cup–winning jersey

Brazil

Pelé, number 10
by chance

Players have not always performed with a number on their back, let alone a name. Introduced during the 1930s in England, systematic numbering was formalised by FIFA at the 1954 World Cup. And it was not until the 1958 tournament in Sweden that the number 10 came to symbolise the team's most creative player, due to a 17-year-old debutant named Pelé and a bureaucratic error by the Brazilian FA. Before the start of the competition, Brazil's football powers sent in the list of selected players, as required, but they forgot to allocate specific jersey numbers to the players. A FIFA delegate from Uruguay took charge, rather obliviously handing the number 3 shirt to the first-choice goalkeeper, Gilmar, and the 10 to the hitherto unknown Pelé. Injured in the run-up to the global gathering, Pelé made his first appearance during the third match against USSR and went on to score six goals in four matches. He scored three times in the 5-2 win over France during the semifinal and twice over Sweden in the final, Brazil winning again 5-2. And so the legend of the number 10 was born. By chance.

MEXICO CITY (MEXICO), AZTECA STADIUM
JUNE 21, 1970
Pelé celebrates in Jairzinho's arms after heading Brazil into a lead in the World Cup final against Italy.

The biggest stadium
of all time

The Estádio Jornalista Mário Filho in Rio de Janeiro, Brazil,
better known as the Maracanã, earned a place in the football
record books during the final of the 1950 World Cup, when
no fewer than 199,854 supporters packed into the stadium.
The capacity of the Maracanã has since been reduced to 76,804.

Italy

Four-time World Cup winners Italy are one of the few teams not to play in the colours of their national flag.

Known by Italian fans as *La Nazionale*, the team was renamed *La Squadra Azzurra* ("the Blue Team") by French journalists during the World Cup in 1938, held in France. Originally, Italy played in white, one of the three colours of their national flag (along with green and red). Their first official international, on May 15, 1910, was played in white against France at the Milan Arena. Italy won 6–2. But just eight months later against Hungary on January 6, 1911, they put on a different colour shirt, a blue shirt. The colour, a seemingly strange pick, was chosen in honour of the Royal Family of the House of Savoy, whose official colour is blue. And Italy haven't looked back, becoming known as the *Azzurri*. All other Italian national teams followed suit, choosing blue as their colour. The white of old is used as a second strip, allowing Italians to remember their sporting origins.

5

GLOBAL HONOURS
4 FIFA World Cups
1 Olympic Games

1

CONTINENTAL HONOUR
1 UEFA European Football Championship

2006
World Cup–winning jersey

1910
First jersey

1934-1938
2-time World Cup–
winning jersey

1968
European Championship–
winning jersey

1982
World Cup–winning jersey

The Balotelli
conundrum

Known for his hijinks during his time at Manchester City (2010 to January 2013), Mario Balotelli has a similar history with the Italian national team. During a friendly against Uruguay on November 15, 2011 at Rome's Stadio Olimpico, the *Azzurri* striker came on at halftime wearing the wrong jersey. He had put on an older shirt, something that posed a problem since the match had been organised to promote the new Puma-designed jersey ahead of Euro 2012. The referee did not take long to notice. At the first stoppage in play following an aerial clash with *La Celeste* captain Diego Perez, the referee asked Balotelli to change into the same shirt as his team-mates.

> "I'm Italian, I feel Italian, I'll always play for the Italian national team."
>
> **Mario Balotelli**

WARSAW (POLAND), NATIONAL STADIUM
JUNE 28, 2012
"Super Mario" strikes his trademark pose after scoring a second against Germany in the Euro 2012 semifinal.

Germany

REUNITED AND MULTI-CULTURAL

Reunited after the fall of the Berlin wall in 1989, the *Nationalmannschaft* took advantage of a new nationality law to become more multi-cultural.

Although the German flag is black, red and yellow, the national team play in 19th century Prussian colours: white with black shorts. A national symbol since the 12th century, the eagle is a reference to the Holy Roman Empire. Separation came after World War II, and from 1949 to 1990 two different jerseys were worn by two different German teams: FRG (west) and GDR (east). In 1974, the World Cup came to West Germany and the two teams played each other in Hamburg. East Germany won 1-0. Although reunification (October 3, 1990) allowed Matthias Sammer, a future European Footballer of the Year winner (in 1996), to become the first East German to play for the *Nationalmannschaft*, the new Germany failed to perform at the very highest level. Euro 1996 still remains the only tournament won since reunification. All three of Germany's World Cups were won by those west of the great divide. Germany's 3-0 defeat by Croatia at the 1998 World Cup forced a complete rethink of the national set-up. The nationality law of January 1, 2000, which granted citizenship to all people born in the country, has allowed young second-generation players such as Boateng, Khedira and Özil to emerge.

4

GLOBAL HONOURS
3 FIFA World Cups
1 Olympic Games (GDR)

3

CONTINENTAL HONOURS
3 UEFA European Football
Championships

1990
FRG
World Cup–winning jersey

1954
FRG
World Cup–winning jersey

1974
FRG
World Cup–winning jersey

1974
GDR
Jersey worn during World Cup

1996
European Championship–
winning jersey

13,
Lucky for some

BERLIN (GERMANY), OLYMPIASTADION
OCTOBER 16, 2012
Wearing 13 on his back, Thomas Müller was named Best Young Player at the 2010 World Cup in South Africa.

All players believe their little superstitions and habits give them an extra edge on the pitch. Few, for example, like to wear the number 13 shirt. In Christianity, Judas is synonymous with the number 13. The betrayer of Jesus was the 13th guest at the table of the Last Supper.

And so it is strange that in Germany, with its two-thirds Christian population, wearers of the number 13 jersey have enjoyed great luck. In 1954, Max Morlock, wearing number 13, scored six goals in five matches at the World Cup in Switzerland. This included the goal that launched the comeback against Hungary in the 4th of July final. The Germans were down 2-0 and went on to win 3-2.

At the 1970 World Cup, Gerd Müller, also wearing 13, scored 10 goals in six matches. Four years later "Bomber 13" scored the winning goal in the final and gave the hosts a 2-1 victory over the Netherlands on July 7, 1974. The goal, his fourteenth and last in the World Cup, saw him overtake Frenchman Just Fontaine's record of 13 (all scored at the 1958 finals). The record stood until 2006 when the Brazilian Ronaldo bagged 15. In 2002, Michael Ballack, with 13 on his back, scored the only goal against the United States in the quarterfinals and against South Korea in the semifinals. Ballack was suspended for the final and Germany lost 2-0 against Brazil on June 30.

At the 2010 World Cup, the number 13 jersey was worn by 20-year-old Thomas Müller, who finished the tournament as joint top-scorer with five goals, and was also named its Best Young Player.

HAMBURG (GERMANY), VOLKSPARKSTADION
JUNE 22, 1974
West Germany skipper Franz Beckenbauer shakes hands with his East German counterpart Bernd Bransch before the only official match ever played between the two nations.

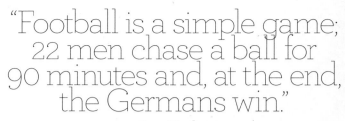

"Football is a simple game; 22 men chase a ball for 90 minutes and, at the end, the Germans win."

Gary Lineker

(England captain and 1986 World Cup Golden Boot winner, after losing the 1990 World Cup semifinal to Germany on penalties)

**MUNICH (GERMANY),
OLYMPIASTADION**

JULY 7, 1974
Gerd Müller is lifted
in triumph after his winning
goal against the Dutch
in the World Cup final.

31

Argentina

ARGENTINIAN ALPHABET

Up until the 1986 World Cup, the Argentinian FA were in the habit of assigning numbers based on players' surnames. The 10 worn by the legendary Maradona was an exception.

When dressing-room superstitions and wheeling and dealing are taken into account, allocating player numbers can be a headache for football authorities. The Argentinian Football Association (AFA) thought it had found a solution to the problem when, during the World Cups of 1974, 1978 and 1982, they distributed numbers in alphabetical order, using players' family names as a guide. Number 1, therefore, went to attacking midfielders Norberto Alonso (also known as "Beto") in 1978 and Ossie Ardiles in 1982, and then to attacker Sergio Almirón in 1986. Goalkeeper Ubaldo Fillol received the 12, followed by the 5 and the 7 (FIFA now insists that number 1 be assigned to a goalkeeper). But there were some exceptions to this very Argentinian rule in 1982. Mario Kempes, number 13 in 1974, should have kept the 10 he wore when his country became world champions in 1978, which would have given Maradona the 12. But the national icon managed to keep hold of the 10, and Kempes wore 11 in the end. The system all but fell apart at Mexico 1986. Captain Daniel Passarella demanded the number 6 jersey that served him so well at club level, while Jorge Valdano wanted the 11. The AFA was eventually forced to give in to the players. It all worked out for the best, however, as the *Albiceleste* went on to lift the prestigious trophy for a second time that year.

5

GLOBAL HONOURS
2 FIFA World Cups
1 FIFA Confederations Cup
2 Olympic Games

14

CONTINENTAL HONOURS
14 Copas América

1986
World Cup–winning jersey

1930
World Cup–runners-up jersey

1978
World Cup–winning jersey

1994
Jersey worn by Maradona
when he scored his last goal
for the national team

2006
First jersey worn by Messi
during a World Cup

From Maradona
to Messi

Suddenly, the Argentinian supporters in Hamburg's World Cup Stadium turned away from their young number 10, Lionel Messi, who was doing his bit to beat a strong Ivory Coast side 2-1 in the opening Group C match of the 2006 finals (June 10). Their eyes were now fixed on another 10, "El Diez." And as the German cameras broadcast the arrival of the great Diego Armando Maradona onto the arena's giant screens, the crowd began long, appreciative chants: "Diego! Diego!"

The match became, in that moment, an afterthought. Until Messi, no player had truly managed to fill Maradona's shoes in the eyes of the Argentinian people, to the extent that on November 14, 2001, more than seven years after awarding him his 91st and final cap in a 2-1 win over Nigeria on June 25, 1994, the AFA decided to retire his number 10 jersey.

After reaching an agreement with the 2002 World Cup Local Organising Committee, the AFA drew up a list of 23 players, numbered 1 to 24. But FIFA rejected it. Article 26, Paragraph 4 of the governing body's regulations requires players to wear the numbers 1 to 23. FIFA President Sepp Blatter suggested giving the 10 to Roberto Bonano, the third-choice goalkeeper, but it was finally allotted to Ariel Ortega, who had already worn the famous number at France 1998. Subsequently, Pablo Aimar and Juan Riquelme took a turn, but it was the emergence of Messi, who made his debut in a friendly with Hungary on August 17, 2005, that would finally solve the "problem." Messi is the only player that Maradona, who inherited the number 10 jersey from the mighty Mario Kempes, sees as his rightful successor in the Argentinian national side.

MEXICO CITY (MEXICO), ESTADIO AZTECA
JUNE 22, 1986
Diego Maradona reaches above England goalkeeper Peter Shilton to punch home his famous "Hand of God" goal for Argentina in the quarterfinal of the World Cup.

After dribbling past 6 opponents and a 60-yard run, Maradona scores the "Goal of the Century."

"Maradona on the ball now. Two closing him down. Maradona rolls his foot over the ball

and breaks away down the right. He goes past a third, looks for Burruchaga.

Maradona forever! Genius! Genius! Genius! He's still going... Gooooal!

Sorry, I want to cry! Good God! Long live football!"

(Victor Hugo Morales's commentary—Radio Continental, Argentina).

Uruguay

To Uruguayan eyes, the presence of four stars on the national jersey seems completely normal, despite the fact that *La Celeste* has only lifted two World Cups.

As is customary in football, each star symbolises a World Cup victory. This small South American nation, boasting a population of just 3.5 million, has two to its name (in 1930 and 1950). However, the reason that FIFA chose Uruguay as hosts for the first-ever World Cup in 1930 was due to their triumphs at consecutive Olympic Games, in 1924 and 1928, the only international football tournament in existence at the time. Uruguayans, therefore, regard this as akin to having won four World Cups. Copying Brazil, the first country to place stars on their jersey in 1970, they added four to their own in 2000. But FIFA amended their rules on April 1, 2010, stating that senior national teams should display a five-pointed star for each World Cup victory, "on the front of the shirt at chest level, immediately adjacent to the Official Member Association Emblem" (Article 16, Chapter 4: Playing Equipment). Uruguay circumvented this new ruling by inserting the stars within the emblem, without placing any outside. *La Celeste* will therefore remain a four-star team for the foreseeable future.

4

GLOBAL HONOURS
2 FIFA World Cups
2 Olympic Games

15

CONTINENTAL HONOURS
15 Copas América

2011
Copa América–winning jersey

1930
World Cup–winning jersey

1950
World Cup–winning jersey

1995
Copa América–winning jersey

2002
Jersey worn at World Cup

Maspoli,
the invisible man

Roque Gaston Maspoli passed away on February 22, 2004, aged 86, in the same way he lived his life: in the shadows. Despite his prestigious career as a Uruguayan international goalkeeper, and then at the helm of Peñarol as the country's most successful club coach, he often had no electricity in his modest Montevideo apartment. He had very little money, but he had known a different type of fortune earlier in life, unexpectedly winning the World Cup in the blink of an eye, on July 16, 1950 in the Maracanã Stadium in Rio de Janeiro. In the 89th minute of Uruguay's final group game against Brazil, an encounter in which the host nation required just a draw to be crowned world champions for the first time, a chance for an equaliser materialised for the home side, who were 2–1 down. But Maspoli raced out to deflect the ball for a corner, thereby sparking off the greatest drama in the history of Brazilian football, henceforth known as the "Maracanaço" (see page 14 for more). The Brazilian attacker foiled by Maspoli had not seen him extend his large (6 ft 2 in.) frame in time. "And do you know why?" the goalkeeper mused before the 2002 World Cup. "Because I never wore bright colours. The eye is attracted to them. By wearing black or brown, forwards had trouble seeing my movements. They also couldn't use me as a visual guide to where the goal was. I'll actually never understand why today's keepers wear luminous colours. After my career ended, I became as invisible as I'd been when I was playing in goal."

"By wearing black or brown, forwards had trouble seeing me."
Roque Gaston Maspoli

RIO DE JANEIRO (BRAZIL), ESTADIO DO MARACANÁ
JULY 16, 1950
Roque Gaston Maspoli tips the ball over the bar for a corner during the decisive match of the World Cup's final group stage against Brazil.

France

World champions for the first time in 1998, France achieved another breakthrough feat on February 22, 2008 by signing the most lucrative national jersey contract ever recorded.

German sportswear manufacturer Adidas had been *Les Bleus'* official jersey supplier since 1972, but they were unable to match the €42.66 million per season offer made by rivals Nike, despite having renegotiated their partnership to the tune of €10 million per year in 2004. The Nike deal, which began on January 1, 2011 and runs until 2018, equates to €320 million over seven and a half years, to which the American company will also add an annual €2.5 million equipment budget for all French national sides, and results-related bonuses. By way of comparison, in April 2006 the Portland-based brand extended its deal to supply Brazil until 2018 for €9.2 million per year (excluding bonuses). Another German manufacturer, Puma, renewed its partnership with Italy in 2005, prior to *La Nazionale*'s fourth World Cup success. The contract, which would have run out in December 2006, now stretches until the end of the 2014 World Cup, and has increased from €9.7 million to €16.25 million per year (including €1.5 million for equipment), which corresponds to €130 million over eight years. Adidas recovered from its French setback by extending the contracts of two of its other historic partners: Spain and Argentina.

4

GLOBAL HONOURS
1 FIFA World Cup
2 FIFA Confederations Cups
1 Olympic Games

2

CONTINENTAL HONOURS
2 UEFA European Football
Championships

FIFA WORLD CUP
FRANCE 98

adidas

F.F.F.

1998
World Cup–winning jersey

1904
First jersey

1909-1914
White jersey with blue
and white stripes

1958
Jersey worn at World Cup

2000
European Championship–
winning jersey

Battiston,
28 years on

When Rogelio Arias, the doctor on duty, discharged him, Patrick Battiston did not hesitate for a second. Relieved and happy to be able to leave, he handed the Spanish medic his jersey, as well as his shorts and socks, in the emergency room of the Seville hospital. Three hours earlier, the French number 3 was lying prostrate on the pitch of Sánchez-Pizjuán Stadium, after being violently clattered by West German goalkeeper Harald Schumacher in the 60th minute of the 1982 World Cup semifinal. Stretchered off while Michel Platini, a good friend and Saint-Etienne team-mate, held his hand, Battiston remained in a groggy state in the dressing room for quite some time. "I only left the stadium in an ambulance during the penalty shoot-out," recalls the former defender. "Once I was at the hospital, a guy in a white coat told me, 'It's alright, you're going to be OK.' And then he said, 'That's a great jersey you've got there.' That's the only memory that I have of that night," he adds. And that remained his only memory, until 2010. Battiston picks up the story: "One morning, one of my two sons received a large package. We were a bit intrigued, but we were blown away when we opened it, as it contained a frame with my jersey inside it! I'd assumed it no longer existed; I'd never have thought that someone would keep it." Or that Rogelio Arias had given it to the Sevilla chairman as a gift. Stopping by the Andalusian outfit in 2008 for a Champions League match, Michel Platini came across it by chance while visiting the club museum. Witnessing the emotion it provoked, the Sevilla chairman decided to offer it to him there and then. Platini, godfather of Battiston's eldest son, had no intention of keeping it, and he sent the jersey back to his old friend immediately. "Getting the jersey back 28 years later is a great footnote to the story," smiles Battiston, delighted at seeing his jersey home at last, given pride of place on his son's bedroom wall.

SEVILLE (SPAIN), ESTADIO RAMÓN SÁNCHEZ PIZJUÁN
JULY 8, 1982
West German goalkeeper Harald Schumacher violently coliding with French defender Patrick Battiston in the semifinal of the World Cup.

(Overleaf)
MARSEILLE (FRANCE), STADE VELODROME
JUNE 23, 1984
Michel Platini runs to celebrate with his team-mates after scoring the winner for France against Portugal in the semifinal of the European Championships.

(Following page)
BRUSSELS (BELGIUM), STADE DU ROI-BAUDOIN
JUNE 28, 2000
Sixteen years later—also against Portugal in the Euro semifinal—Zinédine Zidane impersonates his esteemed predecessor in celebration of his "golden goal" penalty-kick.

Spain

UNITED UNDER THE SAME COLOURS

Before becoming a mighty winning machine, Spain suffered for many years from the rivalry between the Castilians of Madrid and the Catalans of Barcelona.

Spanish football always produced great players, like Alfredo Di Stéfano, who was born in Argentina but played for Spain for most of his life, and won European Footballer of the Year in 1957 and 1959, and Luis Suárez, who won the same award in 1960. But for many years, *La Roja* (as the national team is known) was often relegated to a position of secondary importance in a country defined by regional differences. Undermined by the rivalry between Real Madrid, symbol of the establishment and centralised power, and Catalan representatives Barcelona, whose supporters were hostile to General Franco (1939–1975), the Spaniards rarely played and won together. That changed with the appointment of Madrid-born Luis Aragonés to the helm of the national side in 2004. Taking advantage of an exceptional generation of players led by Iniesta and Xavi, he was able to persuade the Madrid and Barcelona stars to unite with victory as their common goal. After winning Euro 2008, Aragonés made way for the former Real Madrid coach, Vicente Del Bosque, who built on the foundations laid by his predecessor to lead Spain to further glory at the 2010 World Cup and Euro 2012, the first time any nation won three consecutive major international competitions.

2

GLOBAL HONOURS
1 FIFA World Cup
1 Olympic Games

3

CONTINENTAL HONOURS
3 UEFA European Football
   Championships

2012
European Championship–
winning jersey

1950
Jersey worn at World Cup

1964
European Championship–
winning jersey

1984
European Championship–
runners-up jersey

2010
World Cup–winning jersey

Spain

Villa and Ramos
first-name basis

It was not until the 1996–1997 season that UEFA required its clubs to print player names and numbers on the back of their jerseys. Some players, rather than using their full surnames, opted to only display their first name, which was the case for David Villa (Sánchez), Spain's record goalscorer, and his Spanish international team-mate Sergio Ramos (García). So as to distinguish himself from Mali's Mahamadou Diarra, who arrived three years before him at Real Madrid (in 2006), French midfielder Lassana Diarra went for the shortened "Lass." Others approached it differently—at the start of the 1996–1997 campaign, 1991 European Footballer of the Year Jean-Pierre Papin had his initials J.P.P. inserted above the 27 (2+7=9) on his Bordeaux shirt. Waïti, Bordeaux's main sponsor, started offering the J.P.P. jersey free with the purchase of several packs of fruit juice, but the French football authorities soon put a stop to the marketing initiative. To distinguish himself from his father, a former Mexico international (1983–1994) nicknamed "Chicharo" ("the pea") because of his green eyes, Javier Hernández went with "Chicharito" ("the little pea") on his back. Sebastián Abreu, meanwhile, preferred his name to be preceded by "El loco" ("The Madman") on his jersey when he was at Brazilian outfit Botafogo. But Carlos Tevez's attempts to play at the 2010 World Cup as "Carlitos," the name he had sported while at Boca Juniors and Corinthians, were blocked by FIFA. "Kun" Agüero and "Jonás" Gutiérrez were met with the same intransigence. They had taken things just a little too far.

CAPE TOWN (SOUTH AFRICA), GREEN POINT STADIUM
JUNE 29, 2010
David Villa salutes the fans, having just scored against Portugal to propel Spain through to the quarterfinals of the World Cup.

(Following pages)
JOHANNESBURG (SOUTH AFRICA), SOCCER CITY STADIUM
JULY 11, 2010
Andrés Iniesta scores the only goal against the Netherlands to secure Spain's first World Cup.

51

England

In addition to the three lions, taken from the coat of arms of Richard the Lionheart, the England jersey features ten Tudor roses to symbolise the unity achieved in the 15th century.

Since 1966, England have changed their shirts more than 45 times. However, they have worn the coat of arms of Richard the Lionheart since their first match, on November 30, 1872, against Scotland (0-0). Reigning as king between 1189 and 1199, Richard I was the epitome of chivalry and royalty and his coat of arms took the form of three azure lions, one above the other. For the FA, the world's oldest football association (1863), "it was a powerful symbol raised by the throne of England during the Crusades and appropriated by a team heading into combat." To distinguish it from the crest of the cricket team, the FA added the floral emblem of England in 1949. This was a Tudor rose (red with a white centre), the symbol of the unification of the houses of Lancaster (red) and York  (white) that occurred when the Tudor Henry VII married Elizabeth of York, putting an end to the War of the Roses (1455-1485). While the coat of arms used by the England rugby team has only one rose, the football version has ten, one for each league within the FA (in 1949), displayed on a field of silver.

1

**GLOBAL
HONOUR**
1 FIFA World Cup

0

**CONTINENTAL
HONOURS**

1966
World Cup–winning jersey

1872
Jersey worn during the first
international football match

1930
Away jersey,
red since this date

1935
Royal blue jersey

2012
Jersey worn during European
Championship

England

A tradition
dies hard

England likes to stay true to its traditions, including in football. The eleven players that begin a game wear the numbers 1 through 11. So when a regular starter like Rooney is selected as a substitute the number 10 he would normally wear is given to the player on the field. (*)

The first use of numbering in England dates back to August 25, 1928, when Arsenal and Chelsea both had numbers on their shirts when they played against The Wednesday (later renamed Sheffield Wednesday) and Swansea Town, respectively. The initiative did not continue. Following objections that adding numbers to the jerseys was not only too costly but unattractive, the league's governing body rejected a proposal requiring numbered shirts.

As for the England national team, they played with numbers for the first time in a competitive match on April 17, 1937, against Scotland. The numbers were assigned based on the players' positions: one for the goalkeeper, two for the right-back, and so on in ascending order up to the front, right to left, respecting the 2-3-5 formation, and ending with the number eleven, the left winger. The league finally followed suit on June 5, 1939. But with World War II beginning that year the change did not go into full effect until 1946.

The addition of players' names to jerseys happened much more recently. They first appeared on England shirts during Euro 1992 when UEFA made names mandatory. The Premier League then made names and assigning a number obligatory starting from the 1993–1994 season.

ROME (ITALY), STADIO OLIMPICO
OCTOBER 11, 1997
The unforgettable image of Paul Ince's blood-soaked number 4 shirt during a qualifying match for the 1998 World Cup against Italy. FIFA now forces players to change their jerseys should they become bloodied.

(*) In some instances England cannot maintain this policy. Both FIFA and UEFA require players in the final stages of tournaments to keep their shirt number. But as can be seen in the qualifying games for the 2014 World Cup, England are assigning numbers on a match-by-match basis.

Mexico

MEXICO'S NOD TO AZTEC ANCESTORS

Despite being decimated by Spanish invaders, the Aztecs are alive and well in the hearts of Mexicans, who honour their predecessors' founding myth on the national football team crest.

Legend has it that the "Mexica" people, renamed "Aztecs" by the Spanish conquistadors, received an order from one of their gods, Huitzilopochtli, to abandon Aztlan and northern Mexico and settle wherever they found an eagle perched on a cactus, eating a serpent. Eight tribes marched for two hundred years, until one day the prophecy came true in the middle of the swamps. The travellers dried themselves off in 1325 and founded Tenochtitlan, which would eventually become the capital of a massive empire stretching from Texas to Honduras. The fall of Mexico on August 13, 1521 changed nothing. While large Spanish structures were built atop the spongy soil, the myth remained unshakeable for many Mexicans, to the extent that it figures on the national flag and on the jersey worn by *El Tri*, the nickname given to their team in reference to the country's three national colours: green (for hope), white (for purity) and red (for the blood of heroes). When saluting the flag, every player places his right hand by the coat of arms, palm facing down, hoping that a sprinkling of Aztec magic will provide an extra advantage in the 90-minute battle ahead.

2
GLOBAL HONOURS
1 FIFA Confederations Cup
1 Olympic Games

9
CONTINENTAL HONOURS
9 Gold Cups

2013
Home jersey

1930
First jersey worn at World Cup

1978
Away jersey worn
at World Cup

1994
Jersey worn at World Cup

2006
Jersey worn at World Cup

Campos,
Mexico's colour man

When he was not keeping goal for his country, Jorge Campos was scoring goals for his clubs. While the actual figures vary from one Mexican statistician to another, what is clear is that he netted at least 35 in a 16-year career, 14 of those coming in just one season (1989–1990) for Mexican side Pumas. Before earning a reputation as a flying keeper, it was in the role of striker that he excelled while growing up in Acapulco, where he was born on October 15, 1966. But Campos' eccentric streak and taste for the spectacular did not end there. *El Tri*'s legendary custodian also knew how to stand out from the crowd, appearing in some unique kits. During USA 1994, the first of his two World Cup experiences, he made a name for himself globally by wearing a fluorescent pink, green, yellow and red jersey/shorts get-up. The whimsical Mexican got into the habit of coming up with the creative jersey designs himself. His impressive total of 130 caps, amassed between 1991 and November 10, 2004, makes Campos not only one the most colourful goalkeepers of all time, but one of Mexico's best between the posts.

Jorge Campos in some of the eccentric, self-designed goalkeeping jerseys that became his trademark.

USSR

SOVIET STYLE

Before gaining a certain retro cachet, the hammer-and-sickle-stamped jersey draped the backs of the Soviet Union's best footballers as they took on the world.

The iconic red top with "CCCP"—the Cyrillic alphabet's equivalent of "USSR" ("Union of Soviet Socialist Republics")—stamped across it was worn for the first time on August 21, 1923 in Stockholm in a match against Sweden. For a long time, the Soviets were content to test themselves exclusively in the Olympic Games (they won gold in 1956 and 1988), but only when they were not boycotting (as in 1948 in London and 1984 in Los Angeles). They finally made their World Cup debut in 1958. Although the sport was used as political propaganda, the USSR triumphed in just one non-Olympic international tournament, Euro 1960. They lost in the final of three others (the European Championships of 1964, 1972 and 1988). The USSR jersey would be given its final outing on November 13, 1991, in Larnaca, where its wearers defeated Cyprus 3–0. The break-up of the Soviet Union on December 26, 1991 led to the emergence of 15 separate national sides. Russia is considered by FIFA to be USSR's successor, and has inherited those now-defunct teams' results and records. It was a strange decision considering that a majority of the USSR's players came from the other 14 republics, such as Georgia and Ukraine.

2

GLOBAL HONOURS
2 Olympic Games

1

CONTINENTAL HONOUR
1 UEFA European Football Championship

1960
European Championship–
winning jersey

1923
First jersey

1966
Jersey worn at World Cup

1988
European Championship–
runners-up jersey

1991
Last official jersey

Kiev, factory of
champions

A dilapidated two-storey building—demolished to make room for a luxury hotel in 1998—at one time housed some of the gems of Soviet football. But those rising talents, surprisingly, did not belong to one of the powerful Moscow clubs. They were brought through the ranks in the utmost secrecy at Koncha-Zaspa, the training complex belonging to Dynamo Kiev that was founded in 1927 by the forerunners to the KGB. It was there, in a well-to-do suburb of Kiev, that Valeriy Lobanovskyi (1939–2002), known as "The Master," shaped the futures of many great players with an iron hand. Lev Yashin, the only goalkeeper to be named European Footballer of the Year (in 1963), is also the only Soviet winner of the prestigious award to not have been coached by the unsmiling Lobanovskyi. From 1973 to 1990, Lobanovskyi's team ruled over Soviet football, and even managed to transfer that success to the continental stage, defeating Hungarian side Ferencváros 3–0 to lift the European Cup Winners' Cup on May 14, 1975. They also won the same competition again in 1986. That time period saw Dynamo provide a majority of players to the USSR national team, with whom Lobanovskyi enjoyed three separate coaching spells. Two of his players captured the European Footballer of the Year award during his tenure at Dynamo, Oleg Blokhin (in 1975) and Igor Belanov (in 1986). After the fall of the Berlin Wall on November 9, 1989, he had a hand in the development of another future winner, Andrei Shevchenko, who received the accolade in 2004 while playing for A.C. Milan. The year before, Shevchenko laid his hands on the trophy that his mentor had always dreamed of holding: the Champions League.

Left to right (top), and left to right (bottom)
Lev Yashin (the only goalkeeper ever named European Footballer of the Year), Oleg Blokhin (second Soviet player to win the award in 1975), Igor Belanov (1986 European Footballer of the Year) and Andrei Shevchenko (2004's winner).

Cameroon

BIG IDEAS, SHORT SLEEVES

In 2002 and 2004, the Indomitable Lions were as unpredictable with their choice of shirts as they were on the pitch. And their fashion "faux pas" attracted the wrath of FIFA.

In 2000, keen to provide Adidas and Nike with competition, Puma produced several innovative football kits. For Italy, they created a set of tight-fitting jerseys designed to put an end to shirt-pulling. Then at the 2002 African Cup of Nations, they designed sleeveless shirts for Cameroon. FIFA, worried about the lack of space on the sleeves for their logo, banned the top from the World Cup. So Puma added black sleeves. And at the 2004 African Cup of Nations, Puma made the bold move of kitting Cameroon out with their UniQT jersey, a skin-tight, one-piece outfit. FIFA banned the team from wearing it in the quarterfinals, which Cameroon lost. On April 16, 2004, Cameroon were fined €128,900 and had six points deducted from their 2006 World Cup qualifying campaign, before FIFA had a change of heart the very next month and lifted the penalty. FIFA's Law 4, defining the players' equipment, had been found wanting. And it would not be the last time: on July 5, 2012, FIFA, under pressure from the Asian Football Confederation, authorised the wearing of a veil in women's tournaments.

1

**GLOBAL
HONOUR**
1 Olympic Games

4

**CONTINENTAL
HONOURS**
4 African Cups of Nations

2004
UniQt jersey, worn during
the Africa Cup of Nations
(skin-tight one-piece outfit)

1982
First jersey worn at World Cup

1990
Jersey worn at World Cup

2002
African Cup of Nations jersey
vs World Cup jersey

2013
Home jersey

Milla:
an African adventure

Roger Milla was not your average footballer. He was more of a dancer, in football boots. He proved as much at the 1990 World Cup, where Milla was ordered to play by the President of Cameroon. Seventeen minutes after replacing Maboang, the old Indomitable Lion roared in triumph by beating Silviu Lung in the Romanian goal. Milla ran to the corner flag, placed his left hand on his stomach, raised his right hand to the heavens and began to sway this way and that, inventing a dance that caught the attention of the watching world.

"I did it spontaneously. It wasn't planned out," he said. "It's not the Makossa, it's the Milla dance! It's a mix of all kinds of Cameroonian dances." Milla had launched a new craze and ever since then, footballers have tried to imitate him.

Milla headed for the corner flag to dance again after scoring once more in the 86th minute to complete a 2–1 victory. And he scored twice more against Colombia in the first knockout round (in the 106th and 109th minutes of extra time). Thanks to Milla's goals, an African team were in the quarterfinals for the first time (where they would lose 3–2 to England after extra time). Milla returned for the 1994 World Cup and one minute after replacing M'Fédé against Russia on June 28, the fans in San Francisco were on their feet. Milla showed off his dancing skills in front of 75,000 spectators, scoring his team's only goal in a 6–1 defeat. But Cameroon were out. The old lion retired having become the first African to play in three World Cups and the oldest player to play at and score in a World Cup (aged 42 years and 39 days).

> "When I put on this shirt, I become a Lion."
>
> **Roger Milla**

NAPLES (ITALY), STADIO SAN PAOLO
JUNE 23, 1990
Roger Milla celebrates the first of his two goals against Colombia.

Japan

AN EVER-RISING SUN

Made to wait until 1988 to make their first appearance in an international tournament, Japan is now, alongside South Korea, the most formidable footballing nation in Asia.

In Japanese symbolism, the black crow, a figure of family love, is considered good luck. It heralded victory for the samurai and embodied their virtue. Thought to represent the sun, such as the one at the centre of the national flag, the bird's appearance in the empire's official records dates back to approximately 700 AD. The Japanese FA placed a three-legged crow at the heart of the team jersey's crest, its third foot clutching a red ball. But it took its time in bringing luck to the Land of the Rising Sun, as demonstrated by the results of their first two matches, 5–0 and 15–2 defeats to China and the Philippines respectively, on the 9th and 10th of May 1917. The "Samurai Blue" (a neutral colour, with no association to the red and white of the imperial flag) did not actually qualify for an international competition until the Asian Cup of 1988. The launch of the J. League on May 15, 1993 then precipitated the arrival of high-profile foreign players (Bebeto, Lineker, Schillaci and Stoichkov, among others) and managers (Ardiles, Littbarski, Wenger, and more). Reaching their first World Cup in 1998, the Japanese then appeared at the next three. They have been invited to the Copa América three times, their players have well and truly established themselves at European clubs, and the women's team were crowned world champions in 2011, overcoming the United States on penalties after a 2–2 draw.

0

GLOBAL HONOURS

4

CONTINENTAL HONOURS
4 Asian Cups

2011
Asian Cup–winning jersey

1956
Jersey worn
at Olympic Games

1992
First Asian Cup–
winning jersey

1998
First jersey worn
at World Cup

2012
Home jersey

Japan

Nakata:
what's in a name?

The convoy of buses making their way to each match at Perugia's Renato Curi Stadium would often seem endless. Throughout 1999 alone, 30,000 football tourists made the long trip from Japan to profess their admiration for the new emperor, a man named Hidetoshi Nakata. The orange-haired midfielder was not, however, the first Japanese player to try his luck in Europe. But neither Yasuhiko Okudera, the first pioneer (in Germany, 1977–1986), nor Kazu Miura, the first to play in Italy (with Genoa in 1994), shared his head for business. Upon his arrival at Roma, Nakata pocketed $1 million simply by selling a limited series of 1,000 signed jerseys. As the owner of his own image rights via his Sunny Side Up management company, Nakata, who became interested in football after watching the long-running animated football programme Captain Tsubusa when he was a boy, also sold his image to a manga comic, a brand of saké, a video game and more. Perugia would not regret shelling out €2.4 million to Hiratsuka-based club Shonan Bellmare for Nakata in 1998. They sold the creative midfield man to Roma in 2000 for €21.7 million, and the Romans transferred him on to Parma for €30.5 million the following year. Nakata's status as the most expensive Asian in football history is due in part to the fact that, like David Beckham, he was one of the first players to create a link between sport and fashion. In 2000, his name sold more jerseys than any other star save Ronaldo, and in 2004, he earned the same amount as the Brazilian (€16 million). Only Beckham (€30 million) and Zinédine Zidane (€19 million) were bringing in more at the time. He retired early on July 3, 2006, at just 29, in order to travel. But his business sense never left him. On March 30, 2011, a Taiwanese actress paid 27.6 million Yen to purchase a pair of Nakata's signed boots at auction.

NANTES (FRANCE), STADE DE LA BEAUJOIRE
JUNE 20, 1998
Hidetoshi Nakata in action against Croatia in Japan's first World Cup, where they finished last in Group H.

Netherlands

NOT-SO-CLOCKWORK ORANGE

Birthplace of "Total Football," the Netherlands have appeared in three World Cup finals, losing each time.

The Netherlands have historically worn their iconic orange jersey, black shorts and orange socks with pride and panache. The black and orange harken back to the coat of arms of William of Orange, who achieved independence for the United Provinces. But one of the team's nicknames, "Clockwork Orange," stems more from the renowned "Total Football" they perfected than the colours on their backs.

Over the years, however, things have not always gone like clockwork for the Flying Dutchmen. Although they secured their one and only European Championship title in 1988 (2–0 versus USSR, June 25), they were defeated in every one of the three World Cup finals they played in, including two in a row against the host nation in the 1970s (1–2 versus West Germany in 1974; 1–3 a.e.t. vs. Argentina in 1978; and 0–1 a.e.t. vs. Spain in 2010, in South Africa). Only Germany/West Germany have lost more often (four times), but they, at least, also have three triumphs to their name. Twelve different teams have reached the World Cup final through the years, and the *Oranje* are one of just four of them to have never lifted the trophy, alongside Hungary, Czechoslovakia (two finals each) and Sweden (one appearance).

0

GLOBAL HONOURS

1

CONTINENTAL HONOUR
1 UEFA European Football Championship

2010
World Cup–runners-up jersey

1950
First jersey

1974
World Cup–runners-up jersey

1978
World Cup–runners-up jersey

1988
European Championship–
winning jersey

Rep and the case of the stolen jerseys

Johnny Rep was annoyed with himself. He dug around in his sports bag, but his beloved George Best jersey was nowhere to be found. "I was in the habit of wearing it while running training sessions for the little amateur club I coached," recalled the former Dutch winger and veteran of the World Cup finals of 1974 and 1978.

"The jersey came into my possession during his [Best's] testimonial match in 1988 in Belfast. I didn't like hanging on to jerseys at the time—I gave all of them away, including those I got from French stars like Rocheteau, Six, Lopez and Trésor, and even one from Maradona," Rep explained, before saying why he wasn't terribly impressed at getting his hands on the iconic Argentinian's top. "I'd already played in two World Cup finals—1974 and 1978—and I was probably more famous than him at the time!" added Rep, describing the exchange in Berne, Switzerland after a friendly re-match of the 1978 World Cup final. "Maradona was 19 then and he came up to me asking if we could swap shirts. I accepted, but as it didn't really interest me all that much, I gave it away to a friend later."

But Best's shirt was different for Rep, who scored 12 goals in 42 internationals for the Dutch, and many more for club side Ajax. "It actually meant something to me," said Rep, clearly an admirer of the late Northern Ireland and Manchester United winger, before unravelling the mystery. "I found out later that one of my players had stolen Best's jersey from me." Rep continued to explain his earlier ambivalence about jerseys, and how he changed his mind about them later in life. "I was given a huge number of jerseys in my career, and I don't have a single one left," said the man, now 61. "And you know what? I regret it. In 2013, Bastia [his former French club] gave me a special jersey to mark the 30th anniversary of the death of my friend and former French international Claude Papi. But as I was making my way home, my camper van was broken into in Spain, and that jersey was stolen too." He said with a resigned laugh. "I've definitely not had much luck with them."

HANOVER (GERMANY), NIEDER-SACHSENSTADION
JUNE 15, 1974
Johnny Rep (right) is all smiles alongside Johan Neeskens at the final whistle. Rep scored both goals against Uruguay (2–0) in the Netherlands' first game of the 1974 World Cup.

United States

FOOTBALL'S FIRST LADIES

In the United States, the Women's National Team has achieved a level of popularity and notoriety rarely seen in other countries. They are one of just two female national sides, along with Germany, to wear two stars on their jersey.

After the collapse of the NASL, soccer appeared to have had its day in the United States. But the success of women's soccer and the start of a new men's professional league—Major League Soccer—in 1996 helped the sport survive and grow. Now, almost 30 years after the end of the NASL, soccer is thriving and has become an important part of the sporting landscape in the US. Six years after the US Women played their first match on August 18, 1985 (a 1-0 loss to Italy), the team, inspired by Michelle Akers, triumphed in the inaugural 1991 Women's World Cup in China. Since then, the Americans have never finished lower than third in the FIFA tournament and they have secured four of the last five Olympic titles. The success of the 1994 Men's World Cup helped launch MLS, and the league has grown to include 19 teams. The fan support has steadily improved over the years and MLS is now ranked seventh in attendance for all leagues around the world. Although the American women have had the misfortune of witnessing two professional leagues fold, a third, which is being run by the US Soccer Federation and called the National Women's Soccer League (NWSL), began in the spring of 2013. With a new business model and the main goal of sustainability, the league's aim is to help the women's game develop even more in the US. The hope is that Team USA will remain on top of the world and keep adding more stars to their jersey.

GLOBAL HONOURS
2 FIFA Women's World Cups
4 Olympic Games

CONTINENTAL HONOURS
6 Gold Cups

2012
Olympic gold medal–winning jersey

1991
First World Cup–winning jersey

1996
First Olympic gold medal–winning jersey

1999
World Cup–winning jersey

2011
World Cup–runners-up jersey

Women and the beautiful game

Women have played football for almost as long as men, and the women's game has attracted audiences that rival the men's. Indeed, in England, the popularity of women's football in the early 20th century was so great that some say it jeopardized its own future.

One game in particular was pivotal in the history of the women's game. On December 26, 1920, 53,000 fans attended a match at Goodison Park (home to Everton F.C.) featuring Dick, Kerr's Ladies F.C., named after a munitions factory where women worked during World War I. Records indicate that even more fans tried to see the game but were turned away. Within one year women's teams were banned from all FA affiliated grounds. Some players and press have speculated that the decision was made in an effort to keep audiences focused on the men's game.

The ban wasn't lifted until 1969, the same year that the famed Doncaster Belles were founded by lottery ticket sellers at Belle Vue stadium, the home of Doncaster Rovers F.C. The Belles went on to dominate the sport in England winning six FA Women's Cups and reaching the final on a further seven occasions.

Women's football was embraced in other countries, notably within Scandinavia and the US, especially during the second half of the 20th century. Colleges and universities fostered the sport and it flourished in the 1980s with the celebrated North Carolina university team who won 21 of the first 31 women's National Collegiate Athletics Association (NCAA) titles.

One of the iconic images of the 1990s is of the US defender Brandi Chastain jubilant after scoring the decisive penalty against China in the final of the 1999 World Cup (0-0, 5-4 on penalties, July 10). She graced the covers of numerous prestigious publications such as *Time*, *Newsweek* and *Sports Illustrated* propelling the women's game into the limelight once more.

Left to right (top), and left to right (bottom)
North Carolina forward Mia Hamm at Fetzer Field, Chapel Hill, North Carolina (1993); Leonie Maier of Germany (2nd in FIFA's world rankings behind the US) and Shinobu Ohno of Japan (ranked 3rd) during an international friendly at the Allianz Arena in Munich, Germany (June 29, 2013); Ashleigh Mills of Doncaster Rovers Belles during the FA WSL match between Doncaster Rovers Belles and Lincoln Ladies F.C. at the Keepmoat Stadium in Doncaster, England (August 29, 2013); US defender Brandi Chastain on the cover of *Sports Illustrated* (July, 1999).

Sports
Illustrated

YES!

Why Brandi Chastain and the U.S. Women's
Soccer Team Were Unbeatable

A.C. Milan

"IL CLUB PIU TITOLATO AL MONDO" (*)

21 years after saving A.C. Milan from bankruptcy, Silvio Berlusconi saw his grand dreams come true in 2007 as the club became the most trophy-rich team in the world.

"Il club piu titolato al mondo." Following the FIFA Club World Cup final on December 16, 2007, those six words were embroidered in gold on A.C. Milan's jersey, under the crest. This 18th international title propelled the club above Boca Juniors, the Argentinians they just defeated 4-2, meaning Milan now had the most continental and global trophies among all the teams of the world. In addition, it represented the realisation of a long-held dream for Silvio Berlusconi, who had bought the then financially troubled outfit on February 20, 1986. It was a curious fate for a football and cricket (up to 1905) club founded on December 16, 1899 by ten Englishmen and seven Italians whose first president, Herbert Kilpin, was a British vice-consul. Following the English trend at the time, the red and black striped jersey was adopted from the outset. Red for the devil and black to instill fear. Although they have not always been fearsome, A.C. Milan still remain the most successful club on the planet. But they now have to share the accolade again with Boca Juniors, who drew level in trophy count by winning the Recopa Sudamericana in 2008.

(*) The most successful club in the world

18
GLOBAL HONOURS
7 UEFA Champions Leagues
2 UEFA Cup Winners' Cups
5 UEFA Super Cups
3 Intercontinental Cups
1 FIFA Club World Cup

29
NATIONAL HONOURS
18 Italian Leagues
5 Italian Cups
6 Italian Super Cups

1990
UEFA Super Cup–
winning jersey

1963
Champions League–
winning jersey

1969
Champions League–
winning jersey

2003
Home jersey

2007
Champions League–
winning jersey

A.C. Milan

Maldini's
Turkish turmoil

The encounter was not planned. And it nearly turned into a riot. As soon as the A.C. Milan fans caught sight of their players entering Istanbul's international airport, they set about viciously insulting them, venting fury at their heroes' collapse in the UEFA Champions League final against Liverpool the night before, a match *I Rossoneri* lost on penalties after leading 3–0 at the break (May 25, 2005). But, rather than follow the lead of his team-mates who were rushing to get as far away as possible, Paolo Maldini stopped. He turned around, put his bag down and made his way—alone—towards the volatile crowd of supporters. With a piercing glare, he looked right into their eyes and proclaimed: "You are the ones bringing shame on Milan!" The *capitano*, who opened the scoring versus the Reds just a few hours before, spoke at length to the fans, and calm soon reigned. Those fans would not forget the incident or other similar incidents, however. Contrary to Franco Baresi, the previous talismanic Milan captain, Maldini never enjoyed the support of the Ultras in the *Curva Sud*. Holding the opinion that defending the jersey with red and black stripes was the same as defending a certain sporting ethic, the Italian international constantly denounced the violence in which certain football supporters indulged, particularly those who followed his own team. The Ultras had their revenge some four years later, whistling Maldini and displaying banners with hostile messages as he bid farewell to the San Siro. After swearing loyalty to a single jersey for the entirety of his 25-year career, Maldini, a model professional, retired without the respect of a certain section of A.C. Milan's support.

YOKOHAMA (JAPAN), **NISSAN STADIUM,** DECEMBER 16, 2007
A.C. Milan captain Paolo Maldini raises the club's 18th international trophy after helping overcome Boca Juniors in the final of the Club World Cup.

(Following pages)
MILAN (ITALY), SAN SIRO
MAY 4, 2008
Milan's "dream team" from left to right: Clarence Seedorf, Filippo Inzaghi, Kaka, Andrea Pirlo and Massimo Ambrosini.

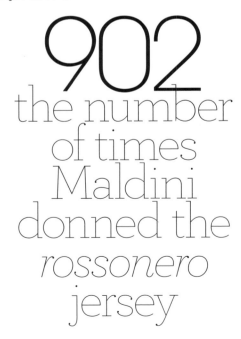

902
the number of times Maldini donned the *rossonero jersey*

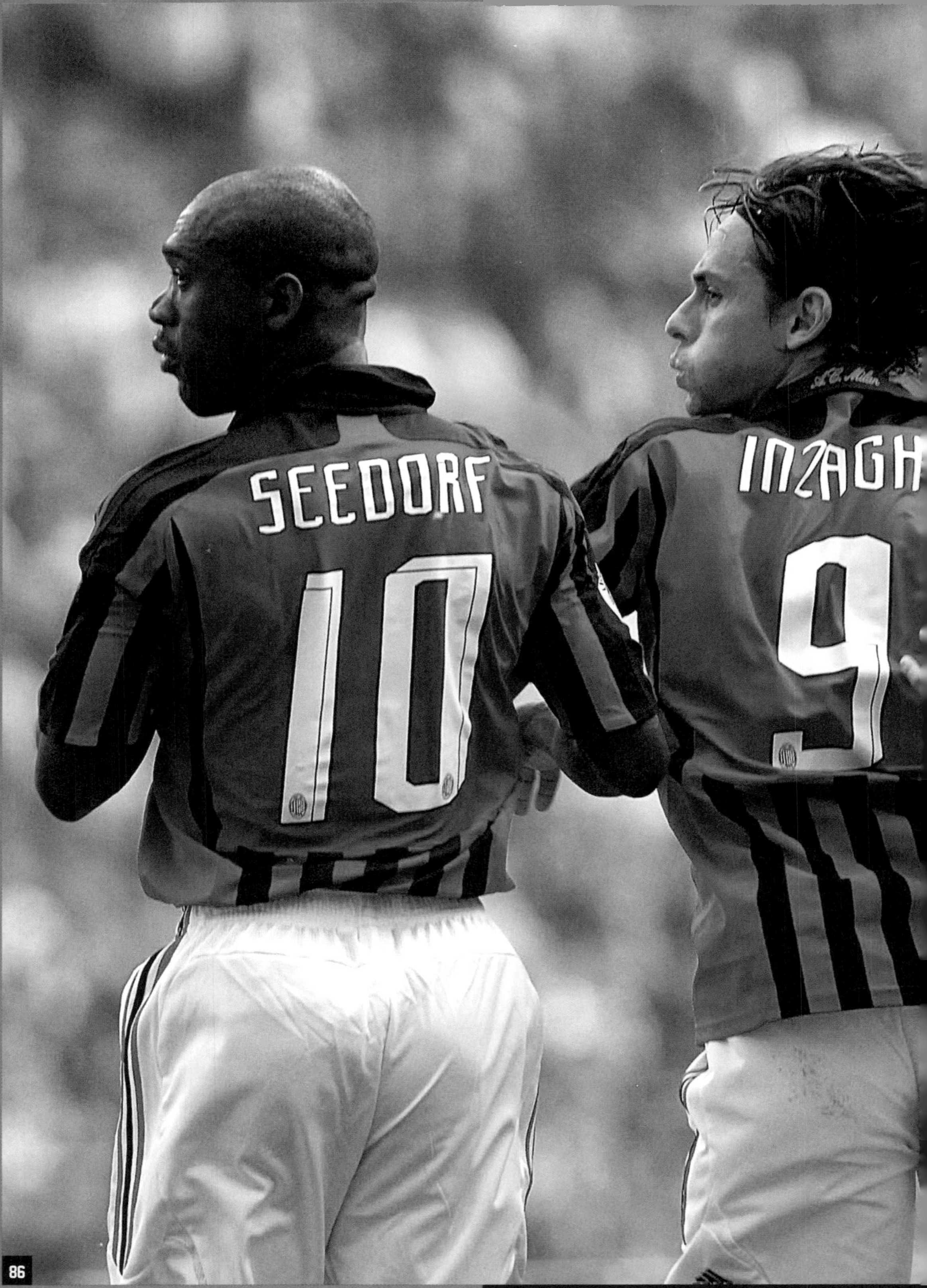
SEEDORF
10
INZAGH
9

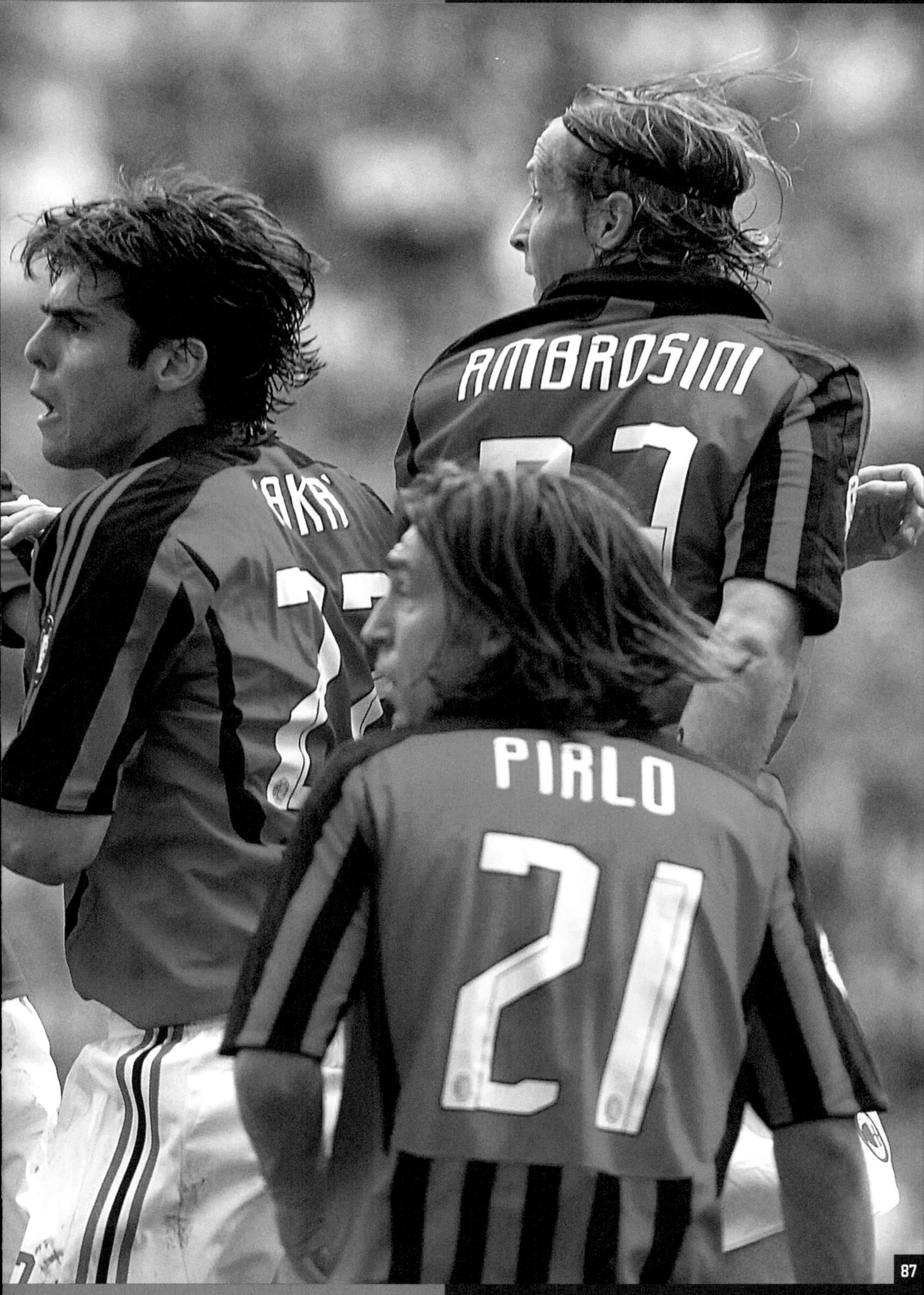
AMBROSINI
PIRLO
21

Boca Juniors

"LA MITAD MÀS UNO" (*)

Founded by factory workers, *Los Bosteros* ("the bumpkins")
state proudly that they are supported by over half of all football
fans in Argentina.

The Genoese immigrants who established the Buenos Aires club on April 3, 1905 kept things simple—they gave it the name of the port district, "La Boca," and added the word "Juniors" as a tribute to football's British roots. Realising that none of the colours they chose (pink, sky blue, or Juventus-style black and white stripes) were suitable, one of them suggested two years later that the club adopt the colours of the next boat that sailed into port. That boat happened to be Swedish, and Boca Juniors' now revered blue and yellow (originally a diagonal yellow stripe, but changed to a horizontal one in 1913) was born. When Mauricio Macri added two white stripes above and below the yellow band upon becoming club president in 1996, Diego Maradona himself threatened to stop wearing the jersey, before later changing his mind.

Coca-Cola was forced to follow suit when *Los Xeneizes* ("the Genoese") asked the company to change the colour of the world-famous logo if it wanted to succeed Pepsi as jersey sponsor in 2004. The reason? Red and white are the colours of River Plate, the club's eternal rivals. Boca's stadium, known as "La Bombonera," thereby became the only place in the world where Coca-Cola's logo is black and white.

(*) Half plus one

18

**GLOBAL
HONOURS**
6 Copas Libertadores
1 Supercopa Libertadores
4 Recopas Sudamericana
3 Intercontinental Cups
2 Copas Sudamericana
...

26

**NATIONAL
HONOURS**
24 Argentinian Leagues
2 Argentinian Cups

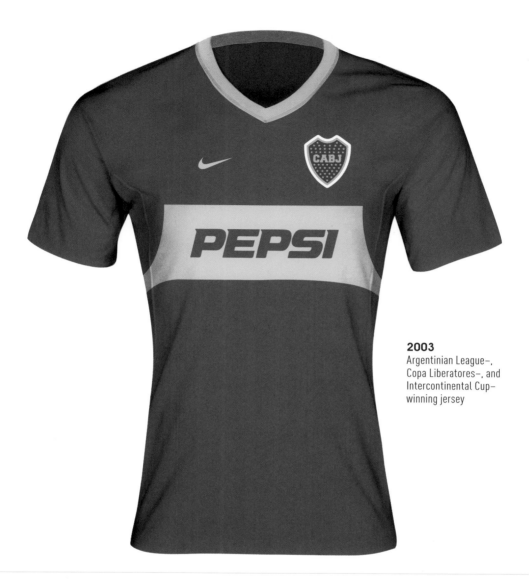

2003
Argentinian League–, Copa Liberatores–, and Intercontinental Cup– winning jersey

1905
First jersey

1907-1912
Blue jersey with a diagonal yellow stripe

1913
Blue jersey with an horizontal yellow stripe

1996
Last jersey worn by Maradona

Riquelme, and the disputed succession

Juan Román Riquelme could not have dreamt of a greater public tribute than the one he got on November 10, 2001, a day earmarked for celebrating the talents of Diego Maradona. Following a gala match organised in his honour at La Bombonera, "El Diez" took off his Argentina jersey to reveal the Boca Juniors equivalent, with number 10 and the name of the man he considered to be his rightful successor printed on its back: Riquelme. Four years earlier, on October 26, 1997, the cultured midfielder, a product of Argentinos Juniors' youth system like Maradona, had already replaced his idol at halftime of a 2–1 *Superclassico* away win over River Plate, Maradona's last official match in Boca colours. He proudly took on his hero's number 10 jersey for six months, before packing his bags for Barcelona, although it was at Villarreal (2003–2007) that he would eventually rise to European prominence. Despite earning 51 caps and scoring 17 goals for Argentina between 1997 and 2008, he never managed to truly fill Maradona's boots, however, even going so far as to quit international football after the 2006 World Cup. Alfio Basile, the new Argentinian coach, persuaded Riquelme to come out of retirement to play a part in beating Chile (2–0) on October 13, 2007, but he definitively shut the door on *La Albiceleste* in March 2009, enraged after being ignored by Basile's successor. The coach in question, who refused to call up the skillful midfield man between October 28, 2008 and the 2010 World Cup, was none other than Maradona! "Riquelme is too slow," he claimed. "El Ultimo Numero Diez," as Riquelme was known, and who had a statue at La Bombonera erected in his honour on July 2, 2011, did gain some semblance of revenge on "El Diez." In 2008, Riquelme was named "Most Popular Player in Boca's History" by fans, receiving 33.37% of the vote compared to Maradona's 26.42%. Riquelme was, perhaps, the rightful successor after all.

A former Boca star (1981–1982 and 1995–1997), Diego Maradona continues to support the club closest to his heart from the balcony of his private box.

Juan Riquelme, seen here battling with River Plate captain Marcelo Gallardo, was named "Most Popular Player in Boca's History" by the club's fans in 2008.

Opened on May 25, 1940, the stadium commonly known as
"La Bombonera" ("The Chocolate Box") earned its nickname
because of its rectangular shape and steep stands.
  Its capacity was increased to 57,395 in 1996 and the ground
offers one of the most intense and passionate atmospheres
in world football.

FC Barcelona

BARÇA: MORE THAN A CLUB

Formed in 1899, FC Barcelona embodies a deep-rooted Catalan identity in Spain, unlike their eternal rivals from the capital, Real Madrid.

The eleven men—six Catalans, two Englishmen, two Swiss and a German—who responded to an advertisement in *Los Deportes* on October 22, 1899 had no way of realising that they were in the process of founding what would become one of the most powerful clubs in the world. The *blaugrana* colours (blue and dark red) were adopted the same year, ahead of a match against Català. And while their crest, shaped like a bowl from 1910 onwards, was the subject of various minor amendments up to 2002, it still takes its inspiration from the coat of arms of the city of Barcelona, which features the St. George's Cross alongside the Catalan flag.

Barça has always conveyed a strong Catalan identity, opposing the centralism of Madrid, to the extent that the club was closed for six months after the Spanish national anthem (*Marcha Real*) was booed and whistled at on June 14, 1925. On August 6, 1936, a month after the start of the Spanish Civil War, then club president Josep Suñol, a Republican and Catalan nationalist, was arrested by forces loyal to General Franco and shot on the spot. Today, Barcelona remains a club that is anchored in its traditions yet still exudes a fearsome modernity.

17

GLOBAL HONOURS
4 UEFA Champions Leagues
3 UEFA Fairs Cups
4 UEFA Cup Winners' Cups
4 UEFA Super Cups
2 FIFA Club World Cups

59

NATIONAL HONOURS
22 Spanish Leagues
26 Spanish Cups
11 Spanish Super Cups

2011
Champions League–
winning jersey

1903
First jersey

1979
First European trophy–
winning jersey
(the Cup Winners' Cup)

1992
First Champions League–
winning jersey

1999
Centenary jersey

FC Barcelona

"Más que una camiseta" (*)

The *blaugrana* jersey had never featured a single advertisement until September 2006, when, for the first time in 107 years of existence, Barcelona struck up an ethical and humanitarian partnership with Unicef, agreeing to display the child-focused organisation's logo on the front of their jerseys. Barcelona even went as far as to pay €1.5 million per year to the United Nations programme, the first time such an arrangement had been considered in football. This was followed by another first, five years down the line, when Barça decided to place a sponsor on their shirts. Offering up to €170 million over six years, or nearly €30 million per season, the Qatar Foundation duly became the club's first official jersey sponsor. However, the contract included a clause enabling Qatar Sports Investments (QSI) to change the brand to be advertised. In line with this, QSI chose to feature Qatar Airways from the start of season 2013–2014. 2014 is also the year in which Doha is scheduled to open its new international airport, predicted to become the second biggest in the world. The Catalans' shirt has become more than a jersey—it is now the symbol of a global club with 350 million supporters worldwide, as well as one of the most sold team shirts on the planet.

After 107 years as a club, Lionel Messi's employers finally put advertising on their jersey in 2006, a decision that now brings Barcelona nearly €30 million per year.

(Following pages)
The Camp Nou, built in 1957, is the largest stadium in Europe, boasting a capacity of 99,354.

(*) More than a jersey

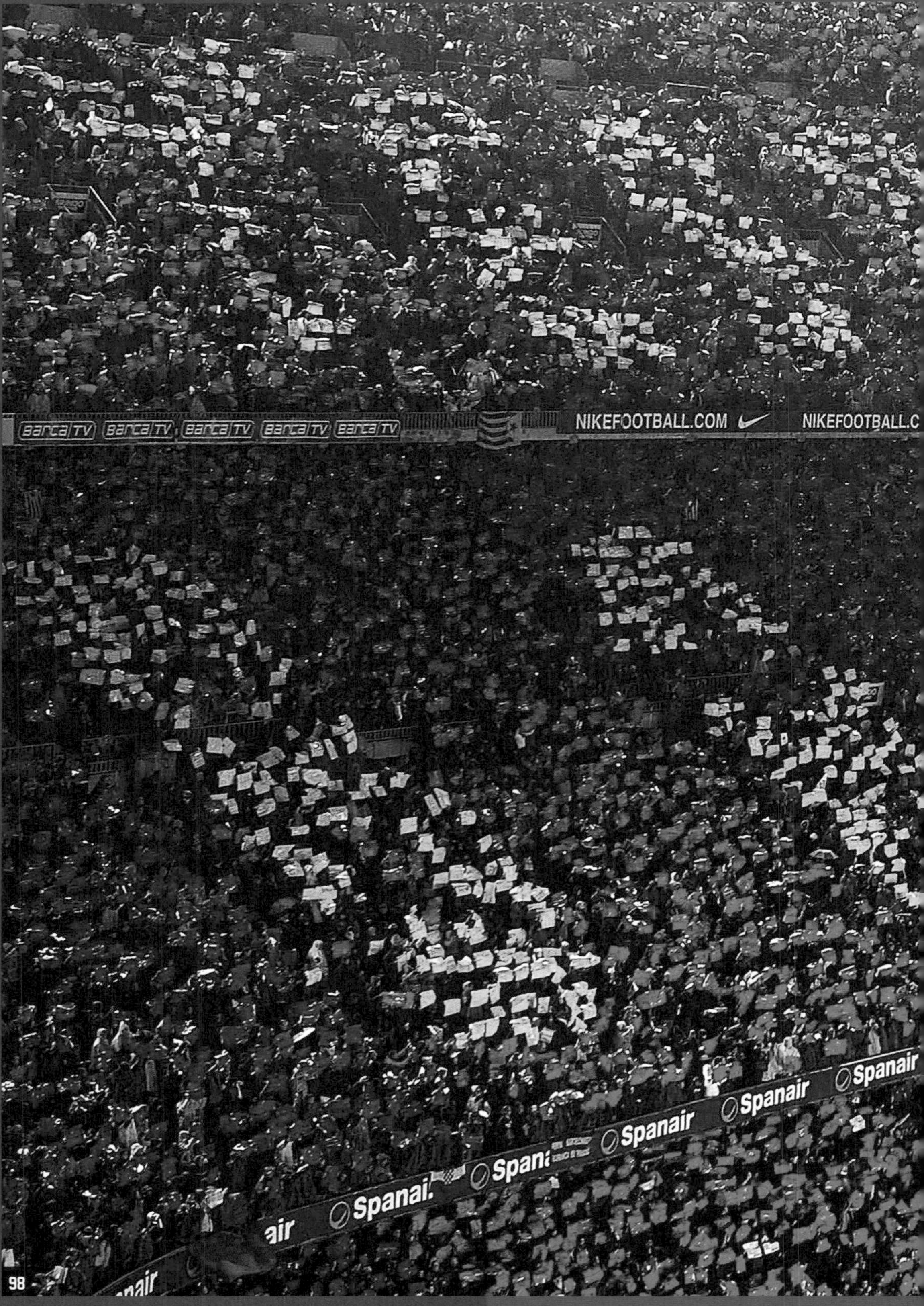
Barça TV
NIKEFOOTBALL.COM
Spanair

Real Madrid

Named "club of the century" by FIFA in 2000, Real Madrid, officially founded on March 6, 1902, did not originally play in the now famous all-white strip.

A blue diagonal stripe, like the one on their crest, appeared across the Spanish club's jerseys in the early days. Captivated by the elegance of London-based side Corinthians, who played in white shirts and trousers, the Real management decided to change to all white. After becoming known as *Los Merengues*, they added buttons as well as the club crest (which remains there to this day) at chest level. The "White House" received royal patronage and became "Real Madrid Club de Fútbol" in 1920, and the crown of Alphonso XIII was added to the top of their crest. It was replaced in 1931 by a blue band representing the region of Castile, upon the establishment of the Second Republic. Madrid regained its "Real Corona" (royal crown) in 1941, two years after the end of the Spanish Civil War. So as to avoid offending the United Arab Emirates, with whom they agreed to open an island theme park in 2015, the club removed the Catholic cross from the crown in their crest in 2012.

15
GLOBAL HONOURS
9 UEFA Champions Leagues
2 UEFA Europa Leagues
1 UEFA Super Cup
3 Intercontinental Cups

59
NATIONAL HONOURS
32 Spanish Leagues
18 Spanish Cups
9 Spanish Super Cups

2012
Spanish League–
winning jersey

1933
Spanish League–
winning jersey

1956-1960
5 times in a row Champions
League–winning jersey

1987
Spanish League–winning
jersey *(Quinta del Buitre*
period)

2000
Champions League–
winning jersey

Zidane:
5 into 10

Zinédine Zidane will go down in football history as a truly great number 10, like Pelé, Maradona and Platini before him. However, he finished his career wearing 5, of all numbers. Upon his arrival in Madrid in 2001, the Frenchman was unable to claim the 10, which already belonged to Portuguese attacking midfielder Luís Figo. Fernando Morientes had the 9 and Steve McManaman had the 8. As for 7, it was the property of Raul. Zidane was then forced to lower his sights and accept one of the traditionally defensive numbers that were still available, opting for the 5. As the unusual number brought him great success, he kept it until the end of his career in 2006, and still makes use of it today to promote his five-a-side football complex in Aix-en-Provence, near his home town of Marseille. A great admirer of Zidane, Brazilian playmaker and 2007 European Footballer of the Year Kaka refused to wear the number 5 when he arrived at Real in 2009 as a mark of respect, choosing 8 instead. Zidane, in fairness, was used to changing numbers. Starting out in Cannes, he wore 11. At Bordeaux, he made do with 7, as the 10 was already taken by Dutch midfielder Richard Witschge. After signing for Juventus, he chose 21 for three reasons: Angelo di Livio wore the 7, the 10 belonged to Alessandro del Piero, and not having to wear 10 helped him avoid being compared to his compatriot, Platini, who was still an idol to the Turin faithful. Even when playing for France, Zidane donned other numbers, making his debut against the Czech Republic (2-2, August 17, 1994) with 14. Whatever his number, his role on the pitch remained that traditionally associated with the number 10—playmaker—and it was from that position that he enthralled an entire planet with his class and skills.

Zinédine Zidane spent five seasons with Real Madrid (2001-2006), where he brought the curtain down on his career.

(Following pages)
From left to right: Captain Raul, Beckham, Figo, Zidane and Samuel. These players all wore the Real jersey together from 2004 to 2005.

Ajax

THE GREEK ORIGINS OF TOTAL FOOTBALL

Ajax's white jersey with a broad red stripe conjures up memories—even today—of some of the most attractive football ever played.

Ajax's fabulous history began in 1893, when a group of friends established "Union," which would become FC Ajax one year later. But the club's official formation date is March 18, 1900, the day they joined the Amsterdam Football Association and established their home pitch in the east of the city, in the Jewish quarter. Since then, their more fanatical supporters call themselves the *Joden* ("Jews" in Dutch), although the club's roots can actually be traced back to Greek mythology rather than Judaism. A Trojan War hero, Ajax was known for his derring-do and bravery. His image has appeared on the club crest since September of 1928. So as to distinguish themselves from rivals PSV Eindhoven and Feyenoord, Ajax changed the colour of their jersey several times, having started out in black with a red sash around the waist. This was replaced by red and white stripes the day after their first league triumph in 1911. They subsequently opted for a white shirt with a wide, vertical red stripe in the middle of the jersey. It was this jersey that would later become the symbol of the "Total Football" approach preferred first by Rinus Michels and then Ştefan Kovács.

The face of mythical hero Ajax first appeared on the club crest on September 20, 1928. It was revised in 1991 with the Gill Sans typeface and redrawn using just eleven strokes to represent the number of players in a football team.

11

GLOBAL HONOURS
4 UEFA Champions Leagues
1 UEFA Europa League
1 UEFA Cup Winners' Cup
3 UEFA Super Cups
2 Intercontinental Cups

58

NATIONAL HONOURS
32 Dutch Leagues
18 Dutch Cups
8 Dutch Super Cups

1992
Europa League–
winning jersey

1911
Jersey worn on club's
promotion to first division

1971
Champions League–
winning jersey

1995
Champions League–
winning jersey

2010
Dutch League–
winning jersey

Cruyff,
from 9 to 14

One of the greatest players of all time, Johan Cruyff did not distinguish himself exclusively with his talent. He also stood out because of the number on the back of his jersey. Starting off with number 9, the "Prince of Amsterdam," his nickname in the city where his mother worked as a cleaner, became known from 1970 onwards for wearing 14, a number traditionally associated with the substitutes' bench. The reason for this unusual choice? While he was injured, his number 9 Netherlands shirt was passed on to Gerrie Mühren. Fully recovered and possibly a little angry at this turn of events, Cruyff did not ask to have the 9 returned to him, deciding to wear the 14 instead. But the tale did not end there. Famous for smoking cigarettes at halftime, he also distinguished himself from other players by slightly altering his kits. The Netherlands national side at the time wore Adidas shorts and an Adidas jersey with three black stripes down the sleeves. But not Cruyff. Having signed a separate sponsorship deal with Puma, the "Flying Dutchman" refused to wear a jersey manufactured by another brand, and played with just two stripes.

This was not an issue during the 1978 World Cup as unfortunately Cruyff did not take part. Victim of a kidnap attempt at his Barcelona residence in 1977, he decided against accompanying his team-mates to Argentina, then run by a military dictatorship. The first player to win three European Footballer of the Year awards (1971, 1973 and 1974), Cruyff had nevertheless already earned his stripes in a remarkable career.

AMSTERDAM (NETHERLANDS), AMSTERDAM ARENA
NOVEMBER 7, 1978
Johan Cruyff wearing a special jersey during his farewell match with Ajax.

GELSENKIRCHEN (GERMANY), PARKSTADION
JUNE 26, 1974
"The Flying Dutchman" wore just two stripes on his kit during the 1974 World Cup, while the rest of his team-mates wore three.

JOHAN CRUYFF

FAREWELL
7-11-78

Liverpool

"YOU'LL NEVER WALK ALONE"

Being part of the Red Army, as Liverpool's supporters are known, is a guarantee of never having to walk alone, as expressed by the anthem and motto of the Merseyside club, founded in 1892.

Players that pull on a Liverpool jersey are aware that they carry a heavy burden. They must honour the memory of the victims of the Heysel Stadium disaster, where 39 supporters died after fences and a retaining wall collapsed on May 29, 1985, and of the Hillsborough disaster, when 96 fans perished following a crush on standing terraces on April 15, 1989.

Liverpool waited until 1896 to drop the blue and white sported by neighbours Everton and adopt a red jersey. The image of a liverbird, a mythical creature—half cormorant, half eagle—used to represent the city of Liverpool was added to the jersey in 1955, and then to the badge in 1987. The twin flames on either side symbolise the Hillsborough memorial outside Anfield. Since 1992, the club motto—"you'll never walk alone"—has appeared above the shield surrounding the liverbird.

11
GLOBAL HONOURS
5 UEFA Champions Leagues
3 UEFA Europa Leagues
3 UEFA Super Cups

48
NATIONAL HONOURS
18 English Leagues
7 FA Cups
8 English League Cups
15 Charity/Community Shields

2005
Champions League–
winning jersey

1892
First jersey

1896
First red jersey

1973
Europa League–winning jersey

2013
Home jersey

Liverpool

Red for victory

What if Liverpool's success was down to the colour of their jersey? To many people, that would seem a terribly simplistic hypothesis to make, but that is exactly what scientific researchers at the English universities of Durham and Plymouth proposed in 2008. According to a study published on March 12 of that year, it is no coincidence that Arsenal (13 titles), Manchester United (20) and Liverpool (18) snap up the majority of the trophies on offer, because teams that play in red win more often. The study found that red jerseys gain an advantage linked to the sensory responses they arouse. In reaching their conclusions, Dr Barton and Dr Hill focused on home matches, when the host teams wear their true colours. What became clear was that teams in red win more often than others. Dr Barton has put forward two possible explanations for this phenomenon: that supporters are unconsciously more attracted to teams wearing red, or alternatively, that red provides a psychological advantage. What the study does not mention is that Liverpool, just like Arsenal and United, possess three of the biggest budgets in the Premier League. It is also worth noting that with their seemingly limitless resources, Chelsea won the title three times during the last decade, and Manchester City were crowned champions in 2012.

TEAMS IN THE ENGLISH LEAGUE BY SHIRT COLOUR (1947–2003)

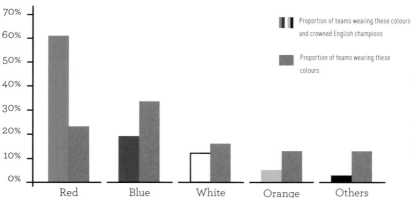

Legend:
- Proportion of teams wearing these colours and crowned English champions
- Proportion of teams wearing these colours

Extract from the study 'Red shirt colour is associated with long-term team success in English football,' carried out by Robert Barton and Russell Hill (March 2008).

ISTANBUL (TURKEY), ATATURK OLYMPIC STADIUM
MAY 25, 2005
Steven Gerrard, Liverpool's talismanic captain, punches the air after the club's victory over A.C. Milan in the Champions League final.

(Following pages)
Liverpool fans celebrate in the famous Anfield Kop.

Juventus

AN OLD LADY WITH AN ENGLISH DRESS SENSE

It was the result of a mistake in England that *La Vecchia Signora* gave up her pink shirts in favour of the iconic stripes now recognised the world over.

On November 1, 1897, thirteen young students met on a bench in Turin to establish a multi-sport club. Aged from 14 to 17, they called it "Sport Club Juventus" ("youth" in Latin). As football strips were not yet readily available, they started off playing in pink, with a tie (or bow tie) and black golf trousers. But as the shirts were of poor quality, they faded quickly. In 1903, they asked Nottingham Forest to deliver some of their red jerseys, but due to a mix-up, black and white striped Notts County F.C. tops were sent back to Italy instead, and Juventus have played in *bianconeri* colours ever since, considering them to be "aggressive and powerful." Juventus became powerful indeed on July 24, 1923, the day Edoardo Agnelli, son of Giovanni, founder of Fiat, purchased the club. Since then, the alliance between the Piedmont upper classes and the southern Italian workers in the Turin-based Fiat factories—who support the team—have enabled the club, renamed "Juventus Football Club" in 1945, to become *La Fidanzata d'Italia* ("The Girlfriend of Italy"). Yet Juventus' special relationship with England has not been forgotten. In 2011 to inaugurate their new stadium Juventus invited none other than Notts County F.C., placed in the third tier of English football, for a friendly match to mark the occasion, an elegant gesture of gratitude for giving them their stripes.

10

GLOBAL HONOURS
2 UEFA Champions Leagues
3 UEFA Europa Leagues
1 UEFA Cup Winners' Cup
2 UEFA Super Cups
2 Intercontinental Cups

44

NATIONAL HONOURS
29 Italian Leagues
9 Italian Cups
6 Italian Super Cups

2003
Champions League–
runners-up jersey

1898
First jersey

1930-1935
"Quinquennio d'oro" jersey
with 5 Scudetti in a row

1984
Italian League and Cup
Winners' Cup–winning jersey

1996
Champions League–
winning jersey

Platini
gave all he had

On May 17, 1987, after bidding farewell to 30,000 fans amassed in the dilapidated Stadio Comunale, Michel Platini headed off into the horizon following an exciting Juventus-Brescia clash (3-2), with good memories but without any of the jerseys he wore throughout his immense career. "I don't even have my last Juventus one," explains the former number 10, voted UEFA's President on January 26, 2007. "I really don't have any left at all, in fact. I've given them all away, to friends, to charitable organisations so that they can bring in some money, and to the many, many people who used to ask me when I was younger."

Platini did hold on to some objects, though. "In fact, I only held on to souvenirs that were round, like two of my three European Footballer of the Year [1983, 1984 and 1985] Ballon d'Or trophies. There's one at Mr Agnelli's house [Giovanni Agnelli, club president while Platini was at Juventus, who passed away on January 24, 2003]. The other two are at home; one's for my son, and the other's for my daughter. Mr Agnelli asked me one day: 'Is it really made out of gold?' I replied, 'Are you mad? I'd never have given it to you if it was! It's just a golden colour.' In return, he gave me a platinum one. The only thing that I kept that wasn't round is the Olympic torch from the Albertville winter games that I carried in 1992. I still have that in my possession."

Michel Platini wore the iconic jersey of Juventus from 1982 to 1987. His coach, Giovanni Trapattoni, said of the Frenchman: "He's a genius, a man born to play football."

(Following pages) Alessandro Del Piero (left), Juventus' all-time leading scorer with 289 goals, and Gianluigi Buffon (right), the club's record transfer (for €54 million in 2001).

Internazionale

INTERNATIONAL OUTLOOK

Founded by dissenting voices from A.C. Milan who disagreed with the club's refusal to field foreigners, Internazionale suffered between the wars under Italy's fascist regime.

Established on March 9, 1908 at the Orologio restaurant by former members of A.C. Milan, Internazionale got its name from the desire of its founders to allow foreign players to join the newly formed team. Milan's refusal to let the 44 Italian and Swiss dissidents play was the principal reason behind their decision to leave the club in order to start up their own. Inter Milan lost their original colours of black and blue in 1928, when the fascist regime, which had prohibited towns from having more than one club, forced them to merge with US Milanese to create an entity known as Ambrosiana, after St Ambrose, the patron saint of Milan. After a 17-year period during which they wore a white jersey with a red cross (the city emblem) they reverted to their original name and colours in 1945. The white shirt would get one more airing, however, as it was used during the 2007–2008 season to celebrate Internazionale's centenary. In 1967, they added a star above the club badge, honouring their ten Italian League titles. In May 2011, the iconic jersey became the first football shirt to go into space, when astronaut Paolo Nespoli took it with him on a mission. From international to interplanetary...

9
GLOBAL HONOURS
3 UEFA Champions Leagues
3 UEFA Europa Leagues
2 Intercontinental Cups
1 FIFA Club World Cup

30
NATIONAL HONOURS
18 Italian Leagues
7 Italian Cups
5 Italian Super Cups

2010
Champions League–,
Italian Cup–, and Italian
League–winning jersey

1910
Italian League–
winning jersey

1928-1945
The 'Ambrosiana' jersey,
white with a red cross

1965
Champions League–
winning jersey

1998
Europa League–
winning jersey

Internazionale

Facchetti,
3 for eternity

Left-back of the renowned *Grande Inter* team (1960–1968) before going on to become club president in 2004, Giacinto Facchetti made a significant impact on the history of the club he loved, and was the first *nerazzurro* player to have his jersey number (3) retired after his death on September 4, 2006 (aged 64). Argentinian defender Nicolás Burdisso, who wore 3 for Inter at the time of Facchetti's passing, was given the number 16 instead.

Retiring a jersey does not necessarily have to be permanent. The number 17 that Marc-Vivien Foé—who died from heart failure during the FIFA Confederations Cup semifinal between Cameroon and Colombia on June 26, 2003—wore when at Lyon was brought back for a fellow Cameroonian in 2008. The honour, which has been bestowed upon fewer than 150 players worldwide, can also be granted to the living. A.C. Milan withdrew the number 6 as a tribute to captain Franco Baresi at the end of his career, as well as the 3 worn by Paolo Maldini. In the future, only Christian and Daniele, the former defender's two sons, will have the right to wear the number 3. Like Santos (Brazil) and the New York Cosmos (USA) did with Pelé, Napoli and Brescia retired the number 10 jersey in honour of Diego Maradona and Roberto Baggio respectively. The 14 has not been allocated at Ajax since April 25, 2007, the date of Johan Cruyff's 60th birthday. Real Madrid may well do the same with their own number 7 jersey one day, now that Cristiano Ronaldo has developed into a veritable brand ("CR7").

The practice of retiring fabled jerseys originates from American sport. The first to do it were the New York Giants American football team in 1935, withdrawing the number 1 worn by Ray Flaherty. One of the most famous examples remains the number 23 worn by Chicago Bulls basketball superstar Michael Jordan. In line with a Japanese tradition, supporters can also be paid hommage in this manner, and numerous clubs have assigned their loyal fans a perpetual number, often the 12.

Giacinto Facchetti in 1971.

Bayern Munich

FROM THE GYM TO FC HOLLYWOOD

Created after splitting from a multi-sport organisation, Bayern Munich have become, in spite of numerous internal problems, one of the most well-supported and powerful clubs in Europe.

On the morning of February 27, 1900, the Munich gymnastics club of MTV 1879 refused to allow its football section to join the German FA (DFB). That very evening, 11 of its members founded FC Bayern Munich ("Bayern" being the German word for "Bavarian"). However, the rise to power of the Nazis in 1933 brought their gradual development to an abrupt halt. Their president and coach, both Jewish, were forced to flee Germany, while Bayern, now referred to as the "Jewish club," battled against ignorance at home. It took them until 1965 to obtain promotion to the Bundesliga, two years after the launch of the professional championship. Despite several high-profile dramas that led to them gaining the nickname "FC Hollywood," the Bavarians have since become one of the most respected, stable and formidable clubs in Europe. Bayern's jersey boasts four stars (see page 158). In order to thank and honour the team's iconic performers of the past, a Bayern "Hall of Fame" was created, featuring 14 Germans as well as Brazilian forward Giovane Elber and French defender Bixente Lizarazu.

10
GLOBAL HONOURS
5 UEFA Champions Leagues
1 UEFA Europa League
1 UEFA Cup Winners' Cup
1 UEFA Super Cup
2 Intercontinental Cups

49
NATIONAL HONOURS
23 German Leagues
16 German Cups
6 German League Cups
4 German Super Cups

2013
German League–
winning jersey

1932
German League–
winning jersey

1967
Cup Winners' Cup–
winning jersey

1974-1976
2-time Champions League–
winning jersey

2001
Champions League–
winning jersey

Bayern Munich

Lizarazu's 69

At the 1954 World Cup finals FIFA required shirt numbers to be allocated to every squad member. Up until then the highest number a shirt would have was 11. When substitutions were introduced to the game in 1965 higher numbers were commonly seen but rarely at the start of a match. Today, of course, that has all changed. The final jersey that French international Bixente Lizarazu wore in his career, from January 2005 to June 2006, is a striking example: the number he chose was none other than 69. "Such an unlikely number, that got a lot of people talking and smiling," recalls Lizarazu. "We've all got our different superstitions—my lucky number is 3. I still sign autographs by adding a little 3. But when I left Bayern for Marseille in 2004, Lucio, the Brazilian centre-back, took it. When I returned to Munich, I was left looking a bit silly, without a number. I started thinking about other numbers; I was looking for something that people would notice and that was fun. And there it was: 69. It's the year I was born, my height and my weight. At least, it was my weight when I started, because at the time I'd already ballooned to 74 kg," he says, laughing. He adds: "No-one had ever dared to do it before in Germany. In marketing terms, it was a masterstroke. But for me, the erotic connotation was not the first meaning that sprang to mind."

The same could not be said of Dino Drpić. Keen to boost sales of his jersey, the Croatian international defender opted for 69 upon his arrival at Karlsruhe in February 2009. But the German League rejected the idea on the pretext that the digits were too difficult to read from far away. Drpić was forced to wear 11 instead. But that was only part of the story. The Balkan defender had chosen the risqué number on the advice of his wife, Nives Celsius, a former Playboy model who previously confessed publicly that she and Drpić had sex on a football pitch in Croatia. By forbidding the 69—on jerseys at least—the German football authorities were likely trying their best to avoid a future scandal. In August 2010, they prohibited the use of any number over 40.

MUNICH (GERMANY), ALLIANZ ARENA
MAY 13, 2006
Frenchman Bixente Lizarazu celebrates his sixth German League title with Bayern Munich.

(Following pages)
The Allianz Arena, here lit up in the red of Bayern Munich, glows blue for 1860 Munich matches and white when the German national team comes to town.

Santos

THE SANTOS SPOTLIGHT

From Pelé to Neymar, Santos has provided a platform for a host of iconic performers through the years. This reputation earned the club a fifth-placed ranking in the FIFA Club of the Century voting in December 2000.

When three men met above a bakery on April 14, 1912 with the intention of forming another football club in São Paulo state, they had no way of knowing they were making history. Santos Futebol Clube, created on that fateful day, would go on to produce and nurture such magicians of the beautiful game as Pelé, Robinho and Neymar.

One of the founders' first tasks was to select a colour for their new club's jersey. His first choice was a shirt with white, blue and gold stripes. But as it proved too complicated to make at the time, Santos opted from March 31, 1913 for black and white stripes, like the ones used at Juventus. Over time, though, they settled on an all-white strip. A third, turquoise jersey was also worn in 2012 to mark the club's centenary. The town of Santos is located near the city of São Paulo, Brazil's economic heart, and boasts the country's largest seaport. For this reason, the club's founders decided to adopt a sea creature, a whale, as its mascot. Although it does not appear on the club crest, Pelé's former employers have long been nicknamed the *Peixe* ("Fish").

8
GLOBAL HONOURS
3 Copas Libertadores
1 Copa CONMEBOL
1 Supercopa Libertadores
1 Recopa Sudamericana
2 Intercontinental Cups

34
NATIONAL HONOURS
8 Brazilian Leagues
20 Campeonatos Paulista
1 Brazilian Cup
5 Torneios Rio – São Paulo

2011
Copa Libertadores–
winning jersey

1912
First jersey

1935
First Campeonato Paulista–
winning jersey

1963
Copa Libertadores–
winning jersey

2012
Away jersey

Neymar's
Romario tribute

Born in the state of São Paulo on February 5, 1992, Neymar da Silva Santos Júnior, better known as Neymar, has become the toast of Brazilian football. Since a young age, the prodigy with the distinctive Mohican hairstyle has been breaking records, and not only out on the pitch. Already a wealthy man at 21, neither his income nor the huge release clause in his new contract with FC Barcelona are likely to shrink any time soon.

But there is one figure that has not risen by all that much: the one on the back of his jersey. Having started out wearing the 7, like Robinho, to whom he is often compared and with whom he played at Santos from January to June 2010, Neymar settled on the 11. "One day," he recalls, "I was asked which number I really liked. I answered '11,' and they gave it to me. I'd always been an admirer of [former Brazil international] Romario, and he wore the 11. From that point on, I started to appreciate the number even more and wear it while playing."

It came as no surprise that when Neymar completed his move from Santos to Barcelona on June 3, 2013 for €57 million it was announced he would be wearing the number 11. However, there have been a few exceptions to Neymar's self-imposed rule. To celebrate Santos' centenary, he donned the number 100 for a match—his 101st personal appearance—against Palmeiras. He then allowed the collector's item to be auctioned off, with the proceeds going to a children's cancer charity. Rather more unusual was the number 360 that he wore against Corinthians in October 2010. A reference to the C360 platform launched by the company CSU CardSystem, one of Santos' sponsors, it turned Neymar into a walking—or running—advertisement. By the next match, he had reverted to his trusty number 11.

Brazilian prodigy Neymar came through the ranks at Santos, where he developed into a major star before signing for FC Barcelona on June 3, 2013.

FC Porto

THE DRAGON, A LIVING MYTH

Portugal's biggest club uses the legendary dragon, which gives its name to their stadium, to strike fear in the heart of opponents.

Founded on September 28, 1893, Futebol Clube do Porto rose to true prominence in 1904 to become Portugal's most successful club. The blue and white colours stem from the desire of those in charge in the early days to bestow their multi-sport club with a strong national identity. To achieve that, they borrowed the colours from the Portuguese royal flag. Originally, the crest was comprised of a blue ball bearing the initials of the name of the club (FCP), to which the coat of arms of the city of Porto was added in 1922 to symbolise the strong bond between club and city. Above sits a dragon on the city walls, defending it from potential invaders. The dragon mythology relays the idea that the inhabitants of Porto never give up and remain motivated by a spirit of conquest. This symbolism is so far-reaching that when the club's new stadium opened on November 16, 2003, it was christened "Estádio do Dragão" (Dragon Stadium). "*A Chama do Dragão*" (the flame of the dragon) has ever since enabled FC Porto to shine brightly in the domestic league as well as in Europe.

The emblem of the Estádio do Dragão

7

GLOBAL HONOURS
2 UEFA Champions Leagues
2 UEFA Europa Leagues
1 UEFA Super Cup
2 Intercontinental Cups

67

NATIONAL HONOURS
27 Portuguese Leagues
16 Portuguese Cups
4 Portuguese Championships
20 Portuguese Super Cups

2004
Champions League–
winning jersey

1935
First Portuguese League–
winning jersey

1987
Champions League–,
Intercontinental Cup–, and
UEFA Super Cup–winning jersey

2002
Home jersey

2011
Portuguese League–,
Portugueuse Cup–, and Europa
League–winning jersey

FC Porto

The unworn jersey?

It is often possible for a player to pose with his new FC Porto jersey and never, or hardly ever, put it on. This is because, contrary to other countries, Portuguese legislation places no restriction on the number of player loans allowed. And just like Benfica, Porto do not hesitate to use their €100 million budget (the largest in the country) to secure as many players as possible. In 2005, Porto had no fewer than 83 players on their books. Since then, that figure has dropped to around 60. This downsizing has enabled the *Dragões* to make up for insubstantial domestic TV rights and to help them compete on the European stage. Masters in the art of speculating on young players, especially those from Latin America, with the aim of selling them on for a significant profit, Porto have developed close ties with influential agents by offering them a percentage of resale prices. In Porto, agents have the ideal shop window in which to showcase their players upon their arrival in Europe. This approach has seen the club sell over 20 players for €10 million or more over the last few seasons. Their most jaw-dropping pieces of business involved Brazilian forward Hulk (pictured), who was sold to Zenit St Petersburg for €60 million on September 3, 2012 and Colombian striker Falcao, transferred to Atletico Madrid for €47 million on August 18, 2011, after being bought for €5.5 million from River Plate two years earlier. But of course, those particular stars actually put on the Porto jersey.

Colombian forward Falcao hops on the back of Brazilian strike-partner Hulk. In addition to their many goals, the dynamic duo earned Porto the handsome sum of €107 million when they were sold in 2011 and 2012 respectively.

Manchester United

THE (VERY) DEAR RED DEVILS

The most trophy-laden side in the history of English football, Manchester United is also a flourishing business. The third richest club in the world boasts the most lucrative shirt sponsorship deal ever made.

Founded in 1878 as Newton Heath LYR F.C. by workers on the Lancashire and Yorkshire Railway, the club swapped their green and gold strip for a red jersey and white shorts in 1902, the same year they were renamed "Manchester United F.C." But the Mancunians did not become the "Red Devils" until much later. Hearing that Salford, a neighbouring rugby league team, used the nickname "Red Devils" at a tournament in France in the 1930s, then-manager Sir Matt Busby decided that the intimidating moniker would suit his "Busby Babes" down to the ground. Since 1967, a red devil armed with a trident stares out proudly from the heart of the club crest. And it is an emblem worth millions. American automotive corporation General Motors recently agreed to pay a record-breaking sum of €415 million over seven seasons starting in 2014–2015 to have their Chevrolet brand displayed on the famous red jersey. But the fans have not forgotten the club's roots. In 2010 thousands of Manchester United supporters arrived at Wembley stadium dressed in green and gold for the Carling Cup final against Aston Villa. The fans wore the original kit to show their dissaproval against higher ticket prices and the general running of the club while still supporting the team, perfectly illustrating the power of a shirt's colours.

7

GLOBAL HONOURS
3 UEFA Champions Leagues
1 UEFA Cup Winners' Cup
1 UEFA Super Cup
1 Intercontinental Cup
1 FIFA Club World Cup

55

NATIONAL HONOURS
20 English Leagues
11 FA Cups
4 English League Cups
20 Charity/Community Shields

2008
Champions League–
winning jersey

1902
First red jersey

1968
Champions League–
winning jersey

1999
Champions League–
winning jersey

2013
English League–
winning jersey

MARADONA GOOD
PELÉ BETTER
GEORGE
BEST

Beckham cannot kick with his left foot, can't head the ball, can't tackle and he doesn't score enough goals. Otherwise he's all right.

If I had been born ugly, you would have never heard of Pelé

In 1969, I gave up women and alcohol. It was the worst 20 minutes of my life.

" I SPENT A LOT OF MONEY ON BOOZE, BIRDS AND FAST CARS. THE REST I JUST SQUANDERED. "

THE LEGEND OF NUMBER 7

It all started in 1961, when Manchester United scout Bob Bishop unearthed a talented 15-year-old by the name of George Best. It took just one training session for the club to sign him. Seven years and six trophies later, Best was named European Footballer of the Year for 1968, and the legend of number 7 was born. The phenomenon went far beyond the scope of football. Capable of absolutely anything on, as well as off, the pitch, the gifted winger was the first true rock star footballer of his era. Ousted by United in 1974, he lapsed into alcoholism, suffered financial ruin and died on November 25, 2005 at the age of 59. A one-time idol of Maradona, Best was given a grand, near-state funeral in Belfast. Bryan Robson then wore the 7 jersey from 1981–1994, before Eric Cantona, the *enfant terrible* exiled from France, revived the legend. Following the sudden retirement of the "King," who was voted best United player of all time by the fans, David Beckham inherited the number. Beckham would in turn hand it down to Cristiano Ronaldo in 2003. When the Portuguese striker joined Real Madrid in 2009, Michael Owen, the 2001 European Footballer of the Year, donned the jersey, but enjoyed less success. The refusal of Japanese international Shinji Kagawa to wear it last year led to Ecuadorian winger Antonio Valencia taking up the mantle. Manchester United fans, however, would love to see a new George Best restore the brilliance of the legendary number 7.

(Following pages) **BARCELONA (SPAIN), CAMP NOU**
MAY 26, 1999
Solskjaer scores to complete an incredible comeback by Manchester United. The "Red Devils" trailed Bayern Munich 0–1 in the 91st minute of the Champions League final before a quick-fire double saw them win 2–1.

Eric Cantona, affectionately known by Manchester United fans as "King Eric."

River Plate

In 2011, the unthinkable happened to Club Atlético River Plate. The outfit, founded on May 25, 1901 and that draws its support from traditionally middle-class areas of Buenos Aires, was relegated for the first time in its impressive history.

La Màquina ("The Locomotive"), a nickname given to River Plate in the 1940s when the team was running away with the Argentinian League, derailed badly on June 26, 2011. For the first time since May 2, 1909, the date of its top-flight debut, River Plate was demoted following an aggregate play-off defeat at the hands of Belgrano (0-2, 1-1). The return leg did not even last the full 90 minutes, as the club's fans invaded the Estadio Monumental pitch towards the end. Aside from the significant damage caused to the stadium, 89 people were injured and another 50 or so were arrested. Once tensions subsided, River Plate fans eventually proved their love for the team's iconic jersey, white with a red diagonal stripe (added by the club's Genoese founders during the Buenos Aires carnival of 1905 for a splash of colour). Supporters turned out in huge numbers to support Los Millonarios in the second division, and they had their loyalty rewarded on June 23, 2012, when River returned to the top tier of Argentinian football by beating Almirante Brown 2-0, courtesy of a brace from French striker David Trezeguet.

5

GLOBAL HONOURS
2 Copas Libertadores
1 Intercontinental Cup
1 Supercopa Libertadores
1 Copa Interamericana

33

NATIONAL HONOURS
33 Argentinian Leagues

1986
Copa Liberatores–
winning jersey

1901-1905
First jersey

1908
Jersey worn on club's
promotion to first division

1920
First Argentinian League–
winning jersey

2012
Away jersey

The chicken
and the lion

It sounds like a story borrowed from Aesop's Fables. The men that ran River Plate, known as *Los Millonarios,* were fed up with being referred to as *Las Gallinas* ("The Chickens"), ever since their unexpected 4-2 defeat by Uruguayan giants Peñarol in the final of the 1966 Copa Libertadores. During their next league match, Club Atlético Banfield supporters released a hen wearing a red ribbon onto the pitch, and the derogatory nickname stuck. In 1986 then club president Hugo Santilli (1983-1989) decided to address the issue by adding the emblem of a lion drawn by Caloi, a famous Argentinian caricaturist, to the chest of the jersey. He also removed the red stripe from the back of the shirt. This change in particular caused uproar among River's supporters, furious that their jersey now looked the same as everyone else's from behind. Curiously, it was while wearing this new-look top that River enjoyed the most successful period in their history, claiming a 13th Argentinian Championship, a maiden Copa Libertadores, a first and only Intercontinental Cup and a Copa Interamericana, all in the space of just two years. Taking over from Santilli, Alfredo Davicce, who ran the club from 1989 to 1997, removed the lion and restored the stripe. And River Plate would have to wait ten years before winning another international trophy. The moral of the tale? Better to be lionhearted than a chicken.

**BUENOS AIRES
(ARGENTINA),
ESTADIO
MONUMENTAL**
JUNE 23, 2012
Thanks to a brace from French ace David Trezeguet against Almirante Brown, River Plate make an immediate return to the Argentinian Primera División a year after being relegated for the first time.

Chelsea

HOW THE PENSIONERS BECAME CHAMPIONS

Long viewed as also-rans in the English game, Chelsea, originally known as "The Pensioners," and renamed "The Blues" in 1952, have become one of the most powerful clubs in the world.

When property developers renovated Stamford Bridge in 1904, they had planned for every eventuality, except local team Fulham's refusal to play there. Forced to conjure up a resident club, they bestowed the name of the adjacent borough on it, and so Chelsea F.C. was born on March 10, 1905. Bluish-green jerseys, taken from the colours of the stable belonging to then chairman the Earl of Cadogan, were chosen. The colours became royal blue in 1912. The club emblem, meanwhile, was modified no fewer than seven times. Originally, a Chelsea Pensioner (the term for former members of the British army housed in a nearby nursing home, the Royal Hospital Chelsea) was depicted on the crest. But the image was removed in 1952, when the "Pensioners" became known as the "Blues." A year later, drawing inspiration from the coat of arms of the Metropolitan Borough of Chelsea, Cadogan's own coat of arms, and that of the former Lords of the Manor of Chelsea, a backwards-facing blue lion holding a staff was added to the jersey. A more realistic lion was used between 1986 and 2005, the club's centenary year. Following the takeover by Russian billionaire Roman Abramovich on July 2, 2003, the crest reverted to the traditional lion, a symbol of the past and of a rosy-looking future.

5

GLOBAL HONOURS
1 UEFA Champions League
1 UEFA Europa League
2 UEFA Cup Winners' Cups
1 UEFA Super Cup

19

NATIONAL HONOURS
4 English Leagues
7 FA Cups
4 League Cups
4 Charity/Community Shields

2012
Champions League–
winning jersey

1905
First jersey

1955
First English League–
winning jersey

1971
First European trophy–
winning jersey
(the Cup Winners' Cup)

1998
Cup Winners' Cup–
winning jersey

Drogba,
a fan of the Blues

A massive portrait of Didier Drogba looks down on the Shed End, the historic wall that supports the south side of Stamford Bridge. It shows him kissing the Chelsea badge on the Allianz Arena pitch, the stage for the Blues' greatest achievement: their capture of the Champions League. It was Drobga who almost single-handedly delivered the mythical trophy to the Chelsea fans on May 19, 2012, equalising with a header in the 88th minute, then putting away his team's last penalty kick in the ensuing shootout against Bayern Munich (1-1, 4-3 on penalties). The image guarantees the Ivorian's eternal presence in the hearts of the London club's supporters. On November 2, 2012, they even voted him the greatest Chelsea player of all time, ahead of living legends such as Frank Lampard, Gianfranco Zola and John Terry. And yet the relationship between Drogba and Chelsea's fan-base got off to a rocky start in 2004, as the latter held the former's initial reluctance about joining the club against him for a long period. This would explain why his number 15 jersey (until the departure of Damien Duff in 2006), and then his 11 (picked up by Brazilian midfielder Oscar in 2012), sold in fewer numbers than those of Lampard or Terry, despite the African striker's habit of buying hundreds of them at the club shop to send back to Abidjan. He was not a collector, though. "I've only got three jerseys framed at home: Zidane's, Ronaldo's and Ronaldinho's," he once said. Drogba would have very much liked to add Messi's to his wall before leaving European football, but after having promised him his shirt before the semifinal of the 2012 Champions League, (2-2, April 24. First leg: 1-0), the Argentinian made a sharp exit as soon as the final whistle sounded. Drogba was likely consoled by the fact that T-shirts featuring his own image still sell like hotcakes in Chelsea's shop. He no longer needs to buy them up himself.

MUNICH (GERMANY), ALLIANZ ARENA
MAY 19, 2012
Scorer of Chelsea's equaliser and their last penalty kick in the shootout of the final against Bayern, Ivorian striker Didier Drogba clutches the London club's first Champions League trophy.

Corinthians

Club of the stars (Garrincha, Rivelino, Sócrates and Ronaldo, among others), Corinthians occupies a special place in the heart and history of the Brazilian people.

When immigrant workers from southern Europe established the club on September 1, 1910, they decided to name it after the touring team from London that had just won six matches on Brazilian soil. And so Sport Club Corinthians Paulista came into being. The largest multi-sport club in São Paulo, it is also one of the most popular. Corinthians claim to have 35 million fans, including former President of Brazil Lula (2003–2011) and Formula 1 drivers Rubens Barrichello and Ayrton Senna (who died in 1994). Their mission statement promises that they will be the team "of the people, by the people and for the people." Although their supporters are nicknamed "*O bando de Loucos*" ("the crazy gang"), their first administrators were rather conservative, choosing a cream-coloured jersey, which would eventually become white over time. It was not until 1954 that the black shirt with thin white stripes made an appearance. As for the crest, although it dates from 1913, it has been touched up since. The current emblem stretches back to 1940, when an anchor and two oars were added to reflect the club's success in nautical sports.

4

GLOBAL HONOURS
1 Copa Libertadores
2 FIFA Club World Cups
1 Recopa Sudamericana

41

NATIONAL HONOURS
5 Brazilian Leagues
27 Campeonatos Paulista
3 Brazilian Cups
1 Brazilian Super Cup
5 Torneios Rio – São Paulo

2012
Copa Libertadores–
winning jersey

1914
First Campeonato Paulista–
winning jersey

1954
Campeonato Paulista–
winning jersey

1990
Brazilian League–
winning jersey

2000
First Club World Cup–
winning jersey

Corinthians

A very democratic
jersey

Putting on a Corinthians jersey at the start of the 1980s was not a trivial matter. It was a political choice. That was the intent of Brazil captain Sócrates, one of the founders of the Corinthians Democracy initiative in November 1981. This ideological movement was launched to challenge the military dictatorship and to offer the players the opportunity to run the club collectively. Gate receipts and TV rights were distributed between all the club's employees and between the players, under the guise of win bonuses. In return, they made the decisions about player recruitment and new coaches, which occurred when Zé Maria, former Corinthians defender and 1970 World Cup winner, was offered the manager's post. They also walked onto the pitch before the final of the 1983 São Paulo State Championship to unfurl a banner which read: "Win or lose, but always within a democracy." This self-management, married to an entertaining brand of football, helped the club enjoy great success both on and off the pitch. "We were fighting for freedom, for a change in our country," explained Sócrates, who sadly passed away on December 4, 2011 at the age of 57. A qualified doctor of medicine with a strong political conscience, and the elder brother of Raï, also a one-time *Seleçao* skipper, Sócrates would often appear on the pitch with the inscription "Democracia Corinthiana" on his jersey, or with messages on his back encouraging people to vote in elections. This mini-republic came to a natural end with the emergence of democracy in Brazil in 1985.

Sócrates celebrates a goal during the Clássico Majestoso between Corinthians and São Paulo in 1982 (right). Much more than a gifted footballer, the "Doctor" was also a man of unshakable political convictions often displayed on his shirt (below).

Borussia Dortmund

A WORKING MAN'S JERSEY

TWO STARS FOR EIGHT TITLES

Unlike with national teams, there are no standardised global rules for displaying stars on club jerseys, and the practice varies from one country to another. Crowned German champions for the eighth time in 2012, Borussia Dortmund promptly added a second star above their crest, while Juventus waited for their 20th league success before doing the same. This is because in Germany, the rule is as follows: one star for four titles, two for eight, three for ten and four for twenty (as have Bayern Munich, Bundesliga champions on 23 occasions).

Borussia Dortmund, Schalke 04's great Ruhr rivals, can trace their roots back to the world of steelworkers and miners, and their colours are a reminder of that heritage.

The group of local steelworkers and miners were so excited to have established the club on December 19, 1909, they forgot to give it a name. Busy clinking overflowing glasses by that point, they decided to call it "Borussia," the name of their favourite beer (Borussia also means "Prussian" in Latin). And so the Ballspielverein ("Ball game") Borussia 1909 Dortmund was born. After starting out in blue and white, BVB 09 (as it was renamed in 1945) later adopted yellow and black—yellow for the overalls worn by its workmen supporters, and black as a tribute to its miner fans. These colours proved to be charmed as, prior to becoming the third German club to hoist the Champions League trophy in 1997 (after Bayern Munich and Hamburg), they were the first to secure European silverware on May 5, 1966 (European Cup Winners' Cup, 2-1 a.e.t. over Liverpool). They were also the first German outfit to be floated on the stock exchange in 2000. After flirting with financial ruin five years later, *Die Schwarzgelben* ("Black and yellows") fought back in style to land a German League and Cup double in 2012.

3

GLOBAL HONOURS

1 UEFA Champions League
1 UEFA Cup Winners' Cup
1 Intercontinental Cup

16

NATIONAL HONOURS

8 German Leagues
3 German Cups
5 German Super Cups

2012
Double-winning jersey
(German League and
German Cup)

1909
First jersey

1966
Cup Winners' Cup–
winning jersey

1997
Champions League–
winning jersey

2013
Home jersey

Borussia Dortmund
The yellow wall

Fans, as well as players, bleed for the shirt in the "Cathedral," as Dortmund's stadium, renowned for its unique atmosphere, is commonly known in Germany. The country's largest arena, it was renamed the Signal Iduna Park (after the naming rights were sold to an insurance company) in December 2005. Crippled with debts to the tune of €118 million at the time, Borussia were forced to sell 75% of their stadium, renting it back for €17 million per year so that they could continue to play there. Built for the sole World Cup held in West Germany and opened on April 2, 1974, it originally boasted a capacity of 54,000. Refurbished numerous times, including for the 2006 World Cup, it has a terrace with space for 27,359 standing fans, 24,454 of which are housed in the Südtribüne. 328 feet wide, 170 feet deep and 131 feet high, it constitutes the largest standing terrace in Europe, and is twice the size of the Anfield kop in Liverpool. What the Germans have come to refer to as *Die Gelbe Wand* ("The yellow wall") has turned the Westfalenstadion, as it is still known among Borussia fans, into one of the most colourful and fiery stadiums in the world.

During the 2003-2004 season, BVB 09 recorded the highest attendance in Europe with an average of 79,647 supporters at each league match. In 2011-2012, only Barcelona attracted more people through their gates.

MUNICH (GERMANY), OLYMPIASTADION
MAY 28, 1997
Andreas Möller lifts the Champions League trophy.

(Preceding pages)
Signal Iduna Park, Borussia Dortmund's stadium, also known as the Westfalenstadion and as the "Cathedral."

> "The yellow wall must have helped us win 20 times during the 2011–2012 season, at home as well as away. For an opponent, coming up against the wall is an unforgettable experience."

Jürgen Klopp, Borussia Dortmund manager

Benfica

Floated on the stock exchange since May 22, 2007 (15 million shares), Benfica, one of Lisbon's two giant clubs alongside Sporting, boast a level of popular support in Portugal that only Porto come close to.

On February 28, 1904, 24 students formed a multi-sport club at the Franco pharmacy on the Rua de Belém, in the south-west of Lisbon. Naming it "Benfica," after one of the city's civil parishes, they decided the team would wear red and white. Their motto—*"E Pluribus Unum"* ("Out of many, one")—was inscribed on the crest, which took the shape of a bicycle wheel (cycling being another sport practised at the Benfica club) surrounding a red and white shield. The same motto also happens to appear on the Great Seal of the United States. Over a century later, on September 29, 2009, Benfica registered its 200,000th *sócio* (paying member) across the world. In the meantime, after having abandoned their policy of only signing Portuguese players in the 1970s, they placed three stars above the club crest, representing the 30th Portuguese League title, attained in 1994. They won their first championship back in 1936, and now have about seventy trophies in their display cabinet.

2
GLOBAL HONOURS
2 UEFA Champions Leagues

64
NATIONAL HONOURS
32 Portuguese Leagues
24 Portuguese Cups
4 Portuguese League Cups
4 Portuguese Super Cups

2010
Portuguese League–
winning jersey

1904
First jersey

1936
First Portuguese League–
winning jersey

1962
Away jersey

1973
Portuguese League–
winning jersey

Benfica

Where eagles dare

The animal world has often inspired club founders pondering over potential crests. A basic method of communication, the chosen beast— often ravenous, carnivorous or wild—is meant to embody the values of a club. Benfica settled on an Iberian Eagle, which symbolises authority, independence and nobility. An eagle named Vitoria ("Victory") is actually released over the Estádio da Luz prior to each home fixture, and is depicted with its wings wide open on the club crest. Benfica are not alone in using an eagle in this way. Italian outfit Lazio do the same before their matches at Rome's Stadio Olimpico, while Palermo's badge displays the white and gold eagle from the town's coat of arms. In Greece, the bird finds itself in great demand. Emblem of the Ecumenical Patriarchate of Constantinople, it figures on the crests of AEK Athens, PAOK Salonika and Doxa Drama. In Turkey, Beşiktaş' eagle is black, like the black on the club's jersey. The same goes for Nice in France, for Pirin Blagoevgrad in Bulgaria and for Spartak Nalchik in Russia, but not for their compatriots of Sibir Novosibirsk, who prefer a blue eagle, as do Crystal Palace (England). Eintracht Frankfurt's eagle is red, while in the Ivory Coast (Africa Sports National), Hungary (Ferencváros) and Morocco (Raja Casablanca), the bird is green. Mexican heavyweights Club América boast a golden eagle, and Manchester City's has its tongue sticking out. National teams are also not averse to using the large bird of prey as a symbol. Mali ("The Eagles") and Tunisia ("The Eagles of Carthage") are just two examples. What all of these jerseys have in common is that their fans are unsympathetic to any attempts to remove the powerful image. When Poland's kit manufacturer replaced their eagle with a less visible variant of the national emblem, fan protests forced them to put it back in its rightful place ahead of Euro 2012, the competition that Poland co-hosted with Ukraine.

"Águia Vitória," the eagle that soars above the stands prior to each match held at the Estádio da Luz, has appeared on the Benfica crest for over a hundred years.

E PLURIBUS UNUM

S.L.B.

Arsenal

VICTORY THROUGH HARMONY AND WHITE SLEEVES

Founded on May 1, 1886, by Scottish workers from the arms manufacturer Royal Arsenal in East London, the club with the motto *"Victoria Concordia Crescit"* ("Victory Through Harmony") has changed its name and shirt numerous times.

Arsenal's initial name was Dial Square F.C. (a reference to a sundial at the factory entrance). The club was later named Royal Arsenal and Woolwich Arsenal. Relegated and on the verge of bankruptcy, the club was bought in 1910, and soon moved to the Arsenal Stadium in Highbury, North London, in 1913, whereupon it was renamed Arsenal F.C. As it was the first London club to gain promotion to the First Division in 1904, club officials were unable to find appropriate jerseys in the London area. Instead, they appealed to Nottingham Forest, who sent them a supply of dark red jerseys, Forest's colour of choice at the time. Over the years, the dark red was significantly lightened, and in 1933 white sleeves were introduced for a home match against Liverpool. The change helped the team stand out against the all-red Liverpool and the now famous white sleeves have featured ever since except for two seasons between 1965 and 1967 when all-red shirts were preferred, and during the 2005–2006 season when Arsenal reverted to their original dark red colours to mark their last campaign at Highbury. Adding white to the sleeves seems to have been a wise decision as throughout the 20th century Arsenal were the best team in England with an average league position of 8.5, just ahead of all-red Liverpool.

2

GLOBAL HONOURS
1 UEFA Europa League
1 UEFA Cup Winners' Cup

37

NATIONAL HONOURS
13 English Leagues
10 FA Cups
2 League Cups
12 Charity/Community Shields

2004
English League–winning
jersey

1906
Home jersey

1931
First English League–
winning jersey

1994
First European trophy–
winning jersey
(the Cup Winners' Cup)

2013
Home jersey

Henry,
Arsenal's 12th man

And suddenly, as if by magic, the statue erected in Thierry Henry's honour on December 10, 2011 on the Emirates Stadium forecourt came to life. The French forward climbed down from his pedestal to take to the pitch and score once again for Arsenal. The fans' wildest dreams had become reality during an amazing FA Cup evening against Leeds (1-0, January 9, 2012). The turn of events cost British bookmakers, who were not convinced by the comeback, the princely sum of €1.2 million. "Titi is a legend here. He left an unforgettable imprint on the history of the club. His goal only serves to further enhance his reputation," said a delighted Arsène Wenger at the time. When his former protégé (1999-2007) came back to Arsenal to keep himself fit during the MLS off-season, the experienced coach offered him a six-week contract. "It was difficult for me to say no," explained the New York Red Bulls front-man, voted greatest Arsenal player of all time and best foreign player to ever grace the Premier League in 2008. Henry wore the number 14 jersey in his first spell with Arsenal, but that now belonged to Theo Walcott. He chose 12, the number on his back when he lifted the World Cup in 1998 and triumphed at the European Championship in 2000. It was in that number that the 35-year-old hit the back of the net against Blackburn (7-1) and Sunderland (2-1). He brought his short assignment to a close by appearing in a seventh match, a 4-0 Champions League loss in Milan on February 16, 2012. And then, the Gunners' all-time leading goalscorer (228 goals) continued on his way. His statue, on the other hand, will remain forever.

Since December 10, 2011, a statue of Thierry Henry has stood outside the Emirates Stadium. It captures the Frenchman doing his traditional goal celebration.

With 228 goals to his name, Thierry Henry is the Gunners' all-time top-scorer.

Olympique de Marseille

STRAIGHT FOR GOAL

Following the motto inscribed on their club crest to the letter, Marseille increased the profile of their jersey by playing an effective style that took France and Europe by storm.

The details of the foundation of Olympique de Marseille are as murky as a bowl of bouillabaisse, the fish stew that originated in the southern French city. Some believe the club was founded in August 1899 by way of a merger between the fencing club "L'Epée" and the "Football Club de Marseille," who are said to have bequeathed the famous "Droit au but" ("Straight for goal") motto, which adorned the badge up until 1935 and then again after 1986. For others, l'*OM*, officially recognised by law on December 12, 1900, was formed in 1892. The club itself has opted for 1899. The colour white was adopted right from the start as a nod towards the purity of the Olympian ideal extolled by Pierre de Coubertin—all of the athletes at the first modern Olympic Games, held in Athens in 1896, were dressed in white. But since 1997 and the return of Adidas as kit supplier (a role the company fulfilled between 1974 and 1994, before being ousted for two seasons), Marseille have constantly changed both their away and third colours. Despite marketing concerns, the home top kept its original white. It also boasts a gold star above the crest, which was added in 1993 to mark Marseille's historic Champions League victory. To date, they remain the only French side to have won Europe's premier club tournament.

DROIT AU BUT

1

GLOBAL HONOUR
1 UEFA Champions League

24

NATIONAL HONOURS
9 French Leagues
10 French Cups
3 French League Cups
2 French Super Cups

1993
Champions League–
winning jersey

1924
First French Cup–
winning jersey

1998
Centenary jersey

2004
UEFA Europa League–
runners-up jersey

2010
French League–
winning away jersey

Papin's
benevolent
streak

A Bordeaux-based friend of Jean-Pierre Papin broke down in tears the day the French striker gave him a case full of jerseys as a present. "I had about 60 of them, including some old Soviet and Yugoslav ones," recalls the 1991 European Footballer of the Year. "I knew he collected football jerseys, and I preferred to see them framed on his wall rather than get eaten by moths," he continues. Papin demonstrated the same type of generosity throughout his career. "The whole point of a jersey is to provide people with pleasure. Players should hand out ten a day to supporters who don't have enough money to buy one. That's what I did, to the extent that people—who I often don't remember giving anything to—still come up to me today to show me them," says the former France international. The five-time French League top goalscorer (1988–1992) did keep one jersey for himself, the one he wore when bidding farewell to Marseille supporters at the Stade Vélodrome on April 25, 1992, a match in which the home side defeated Cannes 2–0. "It's symbolic; in fact, I kept one jersey from six of the clubs I played for, Valenciennes, Bruges, Marseille, Milan, Bayern Munich and Bordeaux. A lack of space means I don't have one from my last club, Guingamp (1998), because I had them transformed into chairs by Laurent Pardo, a French designer. The jerseys were used to upholster the chairs, which I've arranged around the poker table in my house in Arcachon. The only thing I collect is balls. I've got some made of glass, wood, leather and, of course, one made of gold: my Ballon d'Or European Footballer of the Year award. That sits on the living room table, because I want to see it every day!" he concludes with a smile.

Jean-Pierre Papin's acrobatic volleys gave birth to a new French footballing term: "Papinade."

Paris Saint-Germain

NOUVEAU RICHE

PARIS St GERMAIN FOOTBALL CLUB

Logo from 1970 to 1972

Logo from 1992 to 1996

Logo from 2002 to 2013

Parisians dreamt of a big club in the City of Light. The Qataris have been building one since 2011, when they took over Paris Saint-Germain.

Before PSG was rich, it was young. The capital outfit has only been in existence since August 12, 1970, following a merger between Stade Saint-Germain and Paris FC, although the club regards August 27, 1970 as the official formation date, even if some matches were played before that. PSG adopted the blue and red of the city of Paris, combining it with the white of Saint-Germain. After collecting a solid amount of silverware in a relatively short space of time, the second French club—after Marseille—to win a European trophy (the European Cup Winners' Cup, May 8, 1996 vs. Rapid Vienna, 1–0), moved into the fast lane on May 30, 2011. Five years after a first attempt, Qatar Sport Investments (QSI), a sovereign wealth fund managed by Sheikh Tamim ben Hamad Al Thani, Crown Prince of Qatar, returned to buy a 70% controlling stake in the Parisian club. On March 6, 2012, QSI acquired the remaining 30%, becoming the sole shareholder. Since then, just as petrodollars transformed Manchester City from 2008 on, huge amounts of Qatari money have begun to flow in the direction of Paris.

1

GLOBAL HONOUR

1 UEFA Cup Winners' Cup

17

NATIONAL HONOURS

3 French Leagues
8 French Cups
3 French League Cups
3 French Super Cups

2013
French League–
winning jersey

1975
Away jersey worn on club's
promotion to first division

1986
French League–
winning jersey

1994
French League–
winning jersey

1996
Cup Winners' Cup–
winning jersey

Paris Saint-Germain

Ibra, Becks and the numbers game

Zlatan Ibrahimovic posed for press photos on July 18, 2012 at the foot of the Eiffel Tower with a jersey featuring—rather tellingly—just his name. "Nothing's been decided yet in terms of my number," he responded uncomfortably when asked about it that day. "But I'm sure that the staff know what would make me happy..." he added. They did, and Ibrahimovic would finally get to wear the number 10 at club level. Wherever he went, from his first team Malmö on, it was already taken: by Rafael van der Vaart at Ajax, by Alessandro Del Piero at Juventus, by Adriano at Inter Milan, by Lionel Messi at Barcelona and by Clarence Seedorf at A.C. Milan. Unfortunately at PSG the 10 had been the property of Nenê for two years. As for the 9 he previously sported at Malmö, Ajax, Juventus and Barcelona, that belonged to Guillaume Hoarau. "I'll hand it over to him if he asks me in French," promised the gangly striker. While Ibrahimovic's polyglot status was never in doubt, he did not oblige. Instead, he lowered his sights to the number 18. But he had not forgotten his original desire. Despite having scored 18 Ligue 1 goals while wearing the 18 shirt, as soon as Nenê left for the Qatari League, he dropped it in favour of the 10. But this would only be permitted in domestic matches, as UEFA forbids a player from changing numbers in the middle of a season.

The Swede therefore finished the 2012-2013 season wearing 10 in Ligue 1 and 18 in the Champions League. The same headache emerged when David Beckham put pen to paper with PSG on January 31, 2013. The superstar constructed his legend at Manchester United by outstanding performances in the 7 shirt worn by George Best and Eric Cantona, and he also managed to acquire the number during his first loan spell at A.C. Milan. But in Paris, Jérémy Ménez beat him to it. As for the 23, a favourite of his at Real Madrid and Los Angeles Galaxy, it had been assigned to Gregory van der Wiel. Beckham decided on the same trick he'd tried in his second stint at Milan. By reversing the 2 and the 3 he could wear the 32, thereby avoiding another unnecessary numbers war.

Earning an annual salary of €14 million (after tax), Zlatan Ibrahimovic is the highest-paid footballer in France by some distance. That amount is a far cry from the €31,800 (before tax) that was paid by PSG per month to David Beckham (excluding the colossal sums he brought in via image rights and endorsements). The rest of Beckham's salary was donated to local charities.

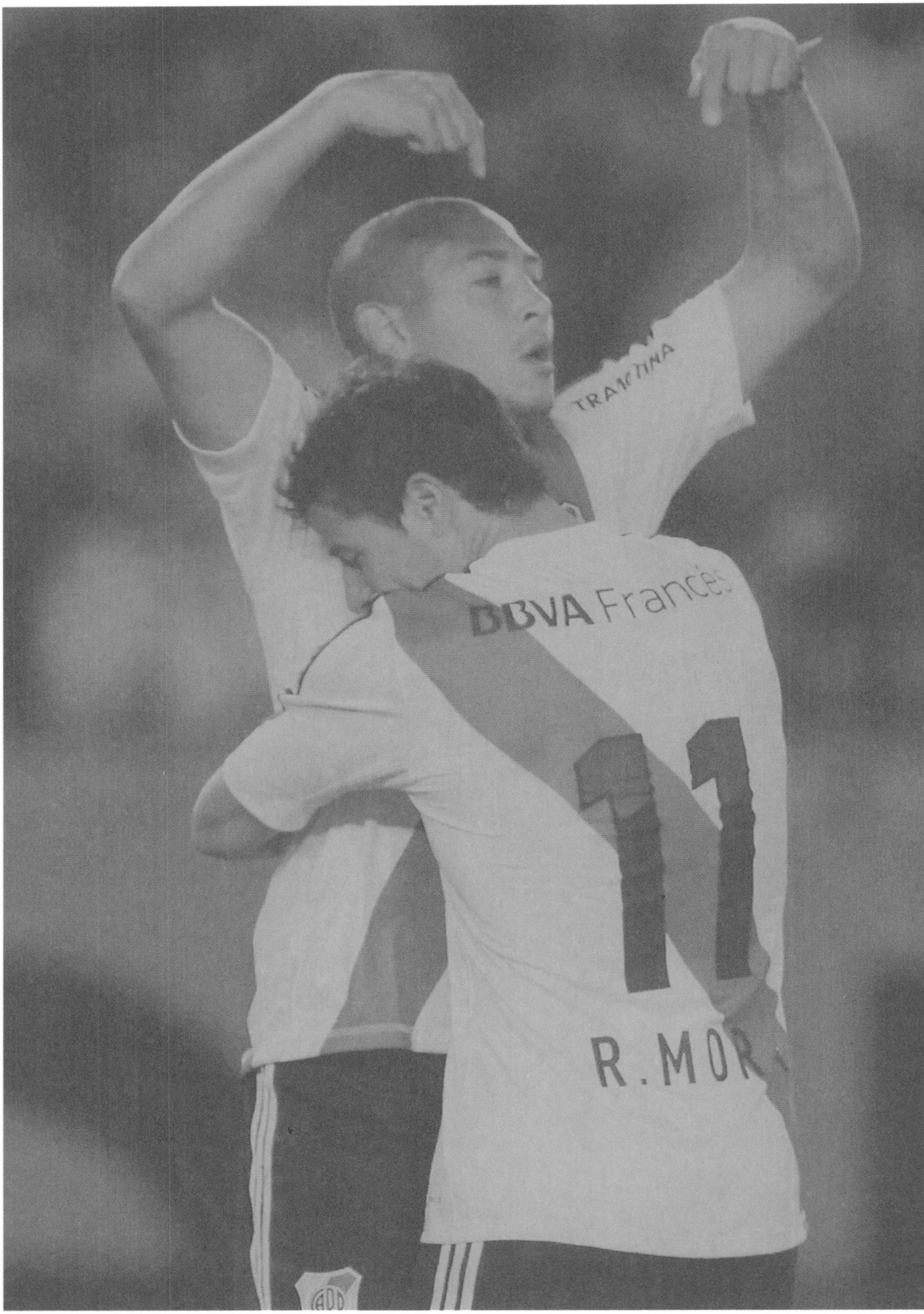
BBVA Francés
11
R.MOR

Spain
Germany
Italy
England
France
Netherlands
Denmark
Sweden
Portugal
Russia
Belgium
Greece
Switzerland
Ukraine
Israel
Norway

850

Football Shirts from Around the World

Brazil
Mexico
United States
Argentina
Colombia
Uruguay
Chile
Ecuador
Ivory Coast
South Africa
Morocco
...

Around the world in 850 jerseys

In the early days of the Beautiful Game, players' shirts were not what they are today. Scraps of wool that distinguished one team from another, they were merely a tool, like the ankle-high boots with studs and long shorts. The only objects that directly represented a club back then were vague novelties and souvenirs.

Football historians have traced the emergence of the first equipment manufacturer back to 1879, before the advent of the professional game. That first manufacturer, Bukta, moved offices to Manchester, in the north of England, in 1885, when lighter cotton shirts began to replace the heavy, unsuitable wool.

It took some time to understand the potential commercial benefits of selling football shirts. They gradually became a way for fans to identify with a club. Wearing such-and-such a jersey was a statement, a courageous commitment, especially in a town or city with more than one club. It also enabled a fan to adopt another persona, to forget his humdrum routine, to be, in a very real sense, a part of the club.

A source of countless fantasies, jerseys finally won over suppliers in 1977, the year shirt sponsorship was approved by the English FA and football is said to have entered its modern age. Since then, football shirts have been transformed into flagship products for brands and lucrative spin-off items for clubs. Manufacturers are constantly redesigning the shirts in the name of merchandising. More appealing, more abundant, more expensive, and coveted throughout the world. Be they collectors' items for aficionados or products to be auctioned online, jerseys have become the golden goose for passionate football fans—and for those businessmen keen to make money catering to them.

The jersey is now sometimes more important than the player. It is not unusual for a club to buy a player based on how many replica jerseys he is likely to sell rather than his ability on the field. It is a piece of kit which has transformed into a fashion accessory.

But, thankfully, the magic remains. Fans watch over the jersey, defending it like guardians of a sacred temple. They feverishly wait for the new version each season, and some dispute the slightest change, considered an affront to the original colours and crest. Football shirts say much about our culture—that's why they fascinate us and differ from one corner of the globe to the next. And this is why the topic deserves a round-the-world overview. Bon voyage, and don't forget your shirt!

the best sellers

clubs selling the most shirts

(average sales per season from 2007 to 2012, source: Dr Peter Rohlmann—October 8, 2012)

MANCHESTER UNITED (ENGLAND)
1.4 MILLION

REAL MADRID (SPAIN)
1.4 MILLION

FC BARCELONA (SPAIN)
1.15 MILLION

CHELSEA (ENGLAND)
910.000

BAYERN MUNICH (GERMANY)
880.000

LIVERPOOL (ENGLAND)
810.000

ARSENAL (ENGLAND)
800.000

JUVENTUS (ITALY)
480.000

INTER MILAN (ITALY)
425.000

A.C. MILAN (ITALY)
350.000

**OLYMPIQUE DE MARSEILLE
(FRANCE)**
350.000

**BORUSSIA DORTMUND
(GERMANY)**
200.000/300.000

MANCHESTER CITY (ENGLAND)
200.000/300.000

PARIS SAINT-GERMAIN (FRANCE)
200.000/300.000

BENFICA (PORTUGAL)
200.000/300.000

the most expensive

clubs with the biggest sponsorship deals
(during 2013-14 season, source: *Huffington Post*—March 5, 2013)

FC BARCELONA (SPAIN)
QATAR AIRWAYS - €30 MILLION

BAYERN MUNICH (GERMANY)
DEUTSCHE TELEKOM - €30 MILLION

PARIS SAINT-GERMAIN (FRANCE)
FLY EMIRATES - €25 MILLION

LIVERPOOL (ENGLAND)
STANDARD CHARTERED - €24 MILLION

MANCHESTER CITY (ENGLAND)
ETIHAD - €24 MILLION

MANCHESTER UNITED (ENGLAND)
AON - €24 MILLION

the best paid

clubs paying the best wages
(during 2012–13 season, source: *France Football*—March 19, 2013)

ANZHI MAKHACHKALA (RUSSIA)
SAMUEL ETO'O - €20 MILLION

PARIS SAINT-GERMAIN (FRANCE)
ZLATAN IBRAHIMOVIC - €15 MILLION

MANCHESTER UNITED (ENGLAND)
WAYNE ROONEY - €13.1 MILLION

MANCHESTER CITY (ENGLAND)
CARLOS TEVEZ - €13.1 MILLION

REAL MADRID (SPAIN)
CRISTIANO RONALDO - €13 MILLION

FC BARCELONA (SPAIN)
LIONEL MESSI - €12.5 MILLION

so wild

when designers let themselves go

COLORADO CARIBOUS (USA)
1978

AJAX (NETHERLANDS)
1990 - AWAY

AUSTRALIA (NATIONAL TEAM)
1991

MANCHESTER UNITED (ENGLAND)
1991 - AWAY

ARSENAL (ENGLAND)
1992 - AWAY

**QUEENS PARK RANGERS
(ENGLAND)**
1992 - GOALKEEPER

READING (ENGLAND)
1992 - AWAY

ATALANTA (ITALY)
1994 - AWAY

BRISTOL ROVERS (ENGLAND)
1994 - AWAY

DERBY COUNTY (ENGLAND)
1994 - AWAY

**EINTRACHT FRANKFURT
(GERMANY)**
1994

HULL CITY (ENGLAND)
1994

MADUREIRA (BRAZIL)
1994

**SHAMROCK ROVERS
(REPUBLIC OF IRELAND)**
1994 - AWAY

CHELSEA (ENGLAND)
1995 - AWAY

NOTTS COUNTY (ENGLAND)
1995 - AWAY

SCUNTHORPE UNITED (ENGLAND)
1995 - AWAY

CROATIA (NATIONAL TEAM)
1996 - GOALKEEPER

ENGLAND (NATIONAL TEAM)
1996 - GOALKEEPER

FC BARCELONA (SPAIN)
1997 - AWAY

JAMAICA (NATIONAL TEAM)
1997

MANCHESTER UNITED (ENGLAND)
1998 - GOALKEEPER

MEXICO (NATIONAL TEAM)
1998

BOCHUM (GERMANY)
1998

MEXICO (NATIONAL TEAM)
1999 - GOALKEEPER

JAGUARES DE CHIAPAS (MEXICO)
2003

ATHLETIC BILBAO (SPAIN)
2004

SAINT-ÉTIENNE (FRANCE)
2005 - GOALKEEPER

**OLYMPIQUE DE MARSEILLE
(FRANCE)**
2008 - AWAY

OLYMPIQUE LYONNAIS (FRANCE)
2011 - AWAY

EVERTON (ENGLAND)
2012 - GOALKEEPER

CHARLEROI (BELGIUM)
2013

RECREATIVO DE HUELVA (SPAIN)
2013 - AWAY

so special

special editions and commemorative shirts

JUVENTUS (ITALY)
1997 - CENTENARY

**OLYMPIQUE DE MARSEILLE
(FRANCE)**
1998 - CENTENARY

FC BARCELONA (SPAIN)
1999 - CENTENARY

ARSENAL (ENGLAND)
2006 - HIGHBURY 1913-2006

INTER MILAN (ITALY)
2008 - CENTENARY

CORINTHIANS (BRAZIL)
2010 - CENTENARY

LAZIO (ITALY)
2010 - 110 YEARS - THIRD

PARIS SAINT-GERMAIN (FRANCE)
2011 - 40 YEARS

FLUMINENSE (BRAZIL)
2012 - 110 YEARS

SANTOS (BRAZIL)
2012 - CENTENARY - THIRD

CELTIC (SCOTLAND)
2013 - 125 YEARS - THIRD

GENOA (ITALY)
2013 - CENTENARY - AWAY

RACING SANTANDER (SPAIN)
2013 - CENTENARY

UNITED STATES (NATIONAL TEAM)
2013 - CENTENARY

PSV EINDHOVEN (NETHERLANDS)
2014 - CENTENARY - AWAY

so vintage

jerseys from days of old

JUVENTUS (ITALY)
1898

FC BARCELONA (SPAIN)
1903

CHELSEA (ENGLAND)
1905

BOCA JUNIORS (ARGENTINA)
1907

BOCA JUNIORS (ARGENTINA)
1908

**BORUSSIA DORTMUND
(GERMANY)**
1909

SANTOS (BRAZIL)
1912

FLUMINENSE (BRAZIL)
1940

MONTERREY (MEXICO)
1945

VÉLEZ SARSFIELD (ARGENTINA)
1945

SOUTH AFRICA (NATIONAL TEAM)
1947

JAMAICA (NATIONAL TEAM)
1948

SPAIN (NATIONAL TEAM)
1950

UNITED STATES (NATIONAL TEAM)
1950

**DUKLA PRAGUE
(CZECH REPUBLIC)**
1960

AS MONACO (FRANCE)
1961

CUBA (NATIONAL TEAM)
1962

AS ROMA (ITALY)
1966

USSR (NATIONAL TEAM)
1966

CONGO (NATIONAL TEAM)
1968

PARMA (ITALY)
1969

PALERMO (ITALY)
1970 - AWAY

ALBANIA (NATIONAL TEAM)
1973

EAST GERMANY (NATIONAL TEAM)
1974

JAPAN (NATIONAL TEAM)
1974

NETHERLANDS (NATIONAL TEAM)
1974

SAINT-ÉTIENNE (FRANCE)
1976

**LOS ANGELES AZTECS
(UNITED STATES)**
1976

**NORTHERN IRELAND
(NATIONAL TEAM)**
1977

BASTIA (FRANCE)
1978

CHEMNITZER FC (GERMANY)
1978

GUATEMALA (NATIONAL TEAM)
1978

**TAMPA BAY ROWDIES
(UNITED STATES)**
1978

FORT LAUDERDALE STRIKERS
(UNITED STATES)
1979

NEW ENGLAND TEA MEN
(UNITED STATES)
1979

CALIFORNIA SURF
(UNITED STATES)
1980 – AWAY

GHANA (NATIONAL TEAM)
1980

MALI (NATIONAL TEAM)
1980

MOZAMBIQUE (NATIONAL TEAM)
1980

SURINAM (NATIONAL TEAM)
1980

MONTREAL MANIC (CANADA)
1981

MEXICO (NATIONAL TEAM)
1982 – AWAY

From
Argentina
to **Z**ambia,
a journey
across
Planet Football

Spain

NATIONAL TEAM
2014 - ADIDAS

NATIONAL TEAM
2013 - AWAY - ADIDAS

ATHLETIC BILBAO
2014 - NIKE

ATLÉTICO MADRID
2014 - NIKE

ATLÉTICO MADRID
2014 - AWAY - NIKE

CELTA DE VIGO
2014 - AWAY - ADIDAS

ELCHE
2013 - ACERBIS

FC BARCELONA
2014 - NIKE

FC BARCELONA
2014 - AWAY - NIKE

GETAFE
2014 - JOMA

GRANADA
2013 - LUANVI

LEVANTE
2013 - KELME

MÁLAGA
2013 - NIKE

MÁLAGA
2013 - AWAY - NIKE

MÁLAGA
2013 - THIRD - NIKE

OSASUNA
2014 - ADIDAS

RAYO VALLECANO
2014 - ERREÀ

RAYO VALLECANO
2013 - AWAY - ERREÀ

RCD DE LA CORUÑA
2014 - LOTTO

RCD ESPANYOL
2014 - PUMA

RCD ESPANYOL
2013 - AWAY - PUMA

REAL BETIS
2013 - MACRON

REAL BETIS
2013 - THIRD - MACRON

REAL MADRID
2014 - ADIDAS

REAL MADRID
2014 – AWAY – ADIDAS

REAL MADRID
2014 – THIRD – ADIDAS

REAL SOCIEDAD
2013 – NIKE

REAL VALLADOLID
2013 – AWAY – KAPPA

SEVILLA
2014 – WARRIOR

SEVILLA
2014 – AWAY – WARRIOR

VALENCIA
2014 – JOMA

VALENCIA
2014 – AWAY – JOMA

VILLARREAL
2013 – XTEP

Germany

NATIONAL TEAM
2014 - ADIDAS

NATIONAL TEAM
2013 - AWAY - ADIDAS

BAYER LEVERKUSEN
2014 - ADIDAS

BAYERN MUNICH
2014 - ADIDAS

BAYERN MUNICH
2014 - AWAY - ADIDAS

BAYERN MUNICH
2014 - THIRD - ADIDAS

BORUSSIA DORTMUND
2014 – PUMA

BORUSSIA DORTMUND
2014 – AWAY – PUMA

BORUSSIA DORTMUND
2014 – THIRD – PUMA

BORUSSIA MÖNCHENGLADBACH
2014 – KAPPA

BORUSSIA MÖNCHENGLADBACH
2014 – THIRD – KAPPA

EINTRACHT BRAUNSCHWEIG
2014 – AWAY – NIKE

EINTRACHT FRANKFURT
2014 – JAKO

EINTRACHT FRANKFURT
2014 – AWAY – JAKO

FC AUGSBURG
2014 – JAKO

FC AUGSBURG
2014 - THIRD - JAKO

FC NÜRNBERG
2014 - ADIDAS

FSV MAINZ 05
2014 - NIKE

FSV MAINZ 05
2014 - AWAY - NIKE

HAMBURGER SV
2014 - ADIDAS

HANNOVER 96
2014 - JAKO

HANNOVER 96
2014 - AWAY - JAKO

HERTHA BSC
2014 - NIKE

HERTHA BSC
2014 - AWAY - NIKE

HOFFENHEIM
2014 - PUMA

SC FREIBURG
2014 - NIKE

SCHALKE 04
2014 - ADIDAS

VFB STUTTGART
2014 - PUMA

VFB STUTTGART
2014 - AWAY - PUMA

VFL WOLFSBURG
2014 - ADIDAS

WERDER BREMEN
2014 - NIKE

WERDER BREMEN
2014 - AWAY - NIKE

WERDER BREMEN
2014 - THIRD - NIKE

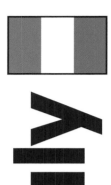

NATIONAL TEAM
2013 - PUMA

NATIONAL TEAM
2013 - AWAY - PUMA

A.C. MILAN
2014 - ADIDAS

A.C. MILAN
2014 - THIRD - ADIDAS

AS ROMA
2014

AS ROMA
2014 - AWAY

ATALANTA
2014 - ERREÀ

ATALANTA
2014 - AWAY - ERREÀ

BOLOGNA
2013 - MACRON

CAGLIARI
2013 - KAPPA

CATANIA
2014 - GIVOVA

CHIEVO
2013 - GIVOVA

FIORENTINA
2013 - JOMA

FIORENTINA
2013 - THIRD - JOMA

GENOA
2013 - LOTTO

INTER MILAN
2014 - NIKE

INTER MILAN
2014 - AWAY - NIKE

JUVENTUS
2014 - NIKE

JUVENTUS
2014 - AWAY - NIKE

JUVENTUS
2013 - THIRD - NIKE

LAZIO
2014 - MACRON

LAZIO
2014 - THIRD - MACRON

LIVORNO
2013 - LEGEA

LIVORNO
2013 - AWAY - LEGEA

NAPOLI
2014 - MACRON

NAPOLI
2014 - AWAY - MACRON

PARMA
2014 - ERREA

PARMA
2014 - AWAY - ERREA

SAMPDORIA
2013 - KAPPA

SASSUOLO
2013 - SPORTIKA

TORINO
2013 - KAPPA

UDINESE
2013 - LEGEA

VERONA
2014 - THIIRD - NIKE

England

NATIONAL TEAM
2013 - NIKE

NATIONAL TEAM
2013 - AWAY - NIKE

ARSENAL
2014 - NIKE

ARSENAL
2014 - AWAY - NIKE

ASTON VILLA
2014 - MACRON

ASTON VILLA
2014 - AWAY - MACRON

CARDIFF CITY
2014 – PUMA

CHELSEA
2014 – ADIDAS

CHELSEA
2014 – AWAY – ADIDAS

CRYSTAL PALACE
2014

EVERTON
2014 – NIKE

FULHAM
2014 – ADIDAS

HULL CITY
2014 – ADIDAS

LIVERPOOL
2014 – WARRIOR

LIVERPOOL
2014 – AWAY – WARRIOR

MANCHESTER CITY
2014 - NIKE

MANCHESTER CITY
2014 - AWAY - NIKE

MANCHESTER UNITED
2014 - NIKE

MANCHESTER UNITED
2014 - AWAY - NIKE

NEWCASTLE UNITED
2014 - PUMA

NEWCASTLE UNITED
2014 - AWAY - PUMA

NORWICH CITY
2014 - ERREÀ

SOUTHAMPTON
2014 - ADIDAS

SOUTHAMPTON
2014 - AWAY - ADIDAS

STOKE CITY
2014 – AWAY – ADIDAS

SUNDERLAND
2014 – ADIDAS

SUNDERLAND
2014 – AWAY – ADIDAS

SWANSEA CITY
2014 – ADIDAS

SWANSEA CITY
2014 – AWAY – ADIDAS

TOTTENHAM HOTSPUR
2014 – UNDER ARMOUR

TOTTENHAM HOTSPUR
2014 – AWAY – UNDER ARMOUR

WEST BROMWICH ALBION
2014 – ADIDAS

WEST HAM UNITED
2014 – ADIDAS

France

NATIONAL TEAM
2014 – NIKE

NATIONAL TEAM
2013 – AWAY – NIKE

AJACCIO
2013 – DUARIG

AJACCIO
2013 – AWAY – DUARIG

AS MONACO
2014 – MACRON

AS MONACO
2014 – AWAY – MACRON

AS SAINT-ÉTIENNE
2014 – ADIDAS

AS SAINT-ÉTIENNE
2014 – AWAY – ADIDAS

ÉVIAN THONON GAILLARD
2013 – KAPPA

ÉVIAN THONON GAILLARD
2013 – AWAY – KAPPA

FC LORIENT
2014 – MACRON

FC LORIENT
2013 – AWAY – MACRON

FC NANTES
2014 – ERREÀ

FC SOCHAUX
2014 – LOTTO

GIRONDINS BORDEAUX
2013 – PUMA

GIRONDINS BORDEAUX
2014 - AWAY - PUMA

GUINGAMP
2014 - PATRICK

LILLE OSC
2013 - UMBRO

LILLE OSC
2013 - AWAY - UMBRO

MONTPELLIER HSC
2014 - NIKE

OGC NICE
2014 - BURRDA

OLYMPIQUE LYONNAIS
2014 - ADIDAS

OLYMPIQUE DE MARSEILLE
2014 - ADIDAS

OLYMPIQUE DE MARSEILLE
2014 - AWAY - ADIDAS

PARIS SAINT-GERMAIN
2014 – NIKE

PARIS SAINT-GERMAIN
2014 – AWAY – NIKE

RENNES
2014 – PUMA

RENNES
2013 – AWAY – PUMA

SC BASTIA
2014 – KAPPA

SC BASTIA
2014 – THIRD – KAPPA

STADE DE REIMS
2013 – HUMMEL

TOULOUSE FC
2014 – KAPPA

VALENCIENNES
2014 – UHLSPORT

Netherlands

NATIONAL TEAM
2013 - NIKE

NATIONAL TEAM
2013 - AWAY - NIKE

ADO DEN HAAG
2013 - ERREA

ADO DEN HAAG
2013 - AWAY - ERREA

AJAX
2013 - ADIDAS

AJAX
2013 - AWAY - ADIDAS

ALKMAAR ZAANSTREEK
2013 - MACRON

FC GRONINGEN
2013 - KLUPP

FC GRONINGEN
2013 - AWAY - KLUPP

FC TWENTE
2013 - NIKE

FC UTRECHT
2013 - HUMMEL

FEYENOORD
2013 - PUMA

FEYENOORD
2013 - AWAY - PUMA

HERACLES ALMELO
2013 - ERIMA

NAC BREDA
2013 - AWAY - PATRICK

NEC
2013 - JAKO

PEC ZWOLLE
2013 - PATRICK

PSV EINDHOVEN
2013 - NIKE

PSV EINDHOVEN
2013 - AWAY - NIKE

SC HEERENVEEN
2013 - JAKO

VITESSE
2013 - NIKE

VITESSE
2013 - AWAY - NIKE

VVV-VENLO
2013 - AWAY - MASITA

WILLEM II
2013 - MACRON

Ukraine

NATIONAL TEAM
2013 - ADIDAS

DNIPRO DNIPROPETROVSK
2013 - THIRD - NIKE

HOVERLA UZHHOROD
2013 - AWAY - ADIDAS

SHAKHTAR DONETSK
2013 - NIKE

VOLYN LUTSK
2013 - AWAY - ADIDAS

FC ZORYA LUHANSK
2013 - NIKE

Belgium

NATIONAL TEAM
2013 - BURRDA

NATIONAL TEAM
2013 - AWAY - BURRDA

AA GENT
2013 - JAKO

ANDERLECHT
2013 - ADIDAS

BEERSCHOT AC
2013 - MASITA

CERCLE BRUGGE
2013 - MASITA

CHARLEROI
2013 - JARTAZI

CLUB BRUGGE
2013 - PUMA

KV MECHELEN
2013 - KAPPA

LIERSE SK
2013 - JAKO

LOKEREN
2013 - AWAY - JARTAZI

OH LEUVEN
2013 - VERMARC

RACING GENK
2013 - NIKE

STANDARD LIÈGE
2013 - JOMA

ZULTE WAREGEM
2013 - PATRICK

Turkey

NATIONAL TEAM
2013 - NIKE

AKHISAR BELEDIYESPOR
2013 - AWAY - NIKE

BESIKTAS
2013 - AWAY - ADIDAS

BURSASPOR
2013 - THIRD - PUMA

BÜYÜKSEHIR BLD. SPOR
2013 - AWAY - NIKE

BÜYÜKSEHIR BLD. SPOR
2013 - THIRD - NIKE

ELAZIGSPOR
2013 - UMBRO

FENERBAHÇE
2013 - ADIDAS

GALATASARAY
2013 - NIKE

GENÇLERBIRLIGI
2013 - THIRD - LOTTO

KASIMPASA
2013 - LOTTO

KAYSERISPOR
2013 - THIRD - ADIDAS

MERSIN IDMANYURDU
2013 - HUMMEL

ORDUSPOR
2013 - AWAY - UMBRO

TRABZONSPOR
2013 - NIKE

Greece

NATIONAL TEAM
2013 - ADIDAS

AEK ATHENS
2013 - PUMA

ARIS SALONIKA
2013 - AWAY - UNDER ARMOUR

ARIS SALONIKA
2013 - THIRD - UNDER ARMOUR

ASTERAS TRIPOLIS
2013 - THIRD - NIKE

ATROMITOS ATHINON
2013 - HUMMEL

LEVADIAKOS
2013 - HUMMEL

OLYMPIACOS
2013 - PUMA

PANATHINAIKOS
2013 - ADIDAS

PANATHINAIKOS
2013 - THIRD - ADIDAS

PANIONIOS
2013 - THIRD - TEMPO

PANTHRAKIKOS
2013 - JOMA

PAS GIANNENA
2013 - THIRD - LOTTO

PLATANIAS
2013 - MACRON

XANTHI
2013 - THIRD

Portugal

NATIONAL TEAM
2014 - NIKE

NATIONAL TEAM
2013 - AWAY - NIKE

ACADÉMICA COIMBRA
2013 - NIKE

BENFICA
2013 - ADIDAS

BENFICA
2013 - AWAY - ADIDAS

CD NACIONAL
2013 - HUMMEL

CS MARÍTIMO
2013 - LACATONI

CS MARÍTIMO
2013 - THIRD - LACATONI

FC PAÇOS DE FERREIRA
2013 - LACATONI

FC PAÇOS DE FERREIRA
2013 - AWAY - LACATONI

FC PORTO
2013 - NIKE

FC PORTO
2013 - THIRD - NIKE

GD ESTORIL PRAIA
2013 - JOMA

GIL VICENTE FC
2013 - THIRD - MACRON

MOREIRENSE
2013 - LACATONI

MOREIRENSE
2013 - AWAY - LACATONI

RIO AVE FC
2013 - LACATONI

SC BEIRA-MAR
2013 - HUMMEL

SC OLHANENSE
2013 - LACATONI

SC OLHANENSE
2013 - AWAY - LACATONI

SPORTING BRAGA
2013 - MACRON

SPORTING CP
2013 - PUMA

SPORTING CP
2013 - AWAY - PUMA

VITÓRIA GUIMARÃES
2013 - THIRD - LACATONI

Romania

NATIONAL TEAM
2013 - ADIDAS

CFR 1907 CLUJ
2013 - JOMA

DINAMO BUCURESTI
2013 - NIKE

OTELUL GALATI
2013 - MASITA

STEAUA BUCURESTI
2013 - NIKE

STEAUA BUCURESTI
2013 - AWAY - NIKE

Russia

NATIONAL TEAM
2014 - ADIDAS

ALANIA VLADIKAVKAZ
2013 - UMBRO

AMKAR PERM
2013 - AWAY - PUMA

ANZHI MAKHACHKALA
2013 - ADIDAS

CSKA MOSCOW
2013 - ADIDAS

DYNAMO MOSCOW
2013 - ADIDAS

FC ROSTOV
2013 - JOMA

KRYLIA SOVETOV
2013 - THIRD - UMBRO

LOKOMOTIV MOSCOW
2013 - PUMA

LOKOMOTIV MOSCOW
2013 - AWAY - PUMA

RUBIN KAZAN
2013 - UMBRO

SPARTAK MOSCOW
2013 - NIKE

SPARTAK MOSCOW
2013 - AWAY - NIKE

TEREK GROZNY
2013 - ADIDAS

ZENIT SAINT PETERSBURG
2013 - NIKE

Czech Republic

NATIONAL TEAM
2013 - ADIDAS

NATIONAL TEAM
2013 - AWAY - ADIDAS

SLAVIA PRAHA
2013 - UMBRO

SLAVIA PRAHA
2013 - AWAY - UMBRO

SPARTA PRAHA
2013 - NIKE

SPARTA PRAHA
2013 - AWAY - NIKE

Switzerland

NATIONAL TEAM
2014 - PUMA

BSC YOUNG BOYS
2013 - JAKO

FC BASEL
2013 - ADIDAS

FC SION
2013 - ERREÀ

FC ZÜRICH
2013 - NIKE

GRASSHOPPERS
2013 - PUMA

Denmark

NATIONAL TEAM
2013 - ADIDAS

NATIONAL TEAM
2013 - AWAY - ADIDAS

AALBORG BK
2013 - ADIDAS

AALBORG BK
2013 - AWAY - ADIDAS

AC HORSENS
2013 - HUMMEL

AGF AARHUS
2013 - HUMMEL

AGF AARHUS
2013 - AWAY - HUMMEL

AGF AARHUS
2013 - THIRD - HUMMEL

BRØNDBY IF
2013 - HUMMEL

BRØNDBY IF
2013 - AWAY - HUMMEL

ESBJERG FB
2013 - NIKE

ESBJERG FB
2013 - AWAY - NIKE

ESBJERG FB
2013 - THIRD - NIKE

FC KØBENHAVN
2013 - ADIDAS

FC KØBENHAVN
2013 - THIRD - ADIDAS

FC MIDTJYLLAND
2014 - WUNDERELF

FC MIDTJYLLAND
2014 - AWAY - WUNDERELF

FC NORDSJÆLLAND
2014 - DIADORA

FC NORDSJÆLLAND
2014 - AWAY - DIADORA

FC VESTSJÆLLAND
2013 - NIKE

ODENSE BK
2014 - PUMA

RANDERS FC
2013 - WARRIOR

SØNDERJYSKE
2013 - DIADORA

VIBORG FF
2013 - KAPPA

Norway

NATIONAL TEAM
2013 - UMBRO

LILLESTRØM SK
2013 - LEGEA

ROSENBORG BK
2013 - ADIDAS

SANDNES ULF
2013 - NIKE

STABÆK FOTBALL
2013 - LEGEA

TROMSØ IL
2013 - PUMA

Israel

NATIONAL TEAM
2013 - ADIDAS

HAPOËL TEL AVIV
2014 - KAPPA

HAPOËL TEL AVIV
2014 - THIRD - KAPPA

MACCABI HAÏFA
2014 - NIKE

MACCABI TEL AVIV
2014 - MACRON

MACCABI TEL AVIV
2014 - THIRD - MACRON

Sweden

NATIONAL TEAM
2013 - ADIDAS

NATIONAL TEAM
2013 - AWAY - ADIDAS

AIK
2013 - ADIDAS

AIK
2013 - AWAY - ADIDAS

ÅTVIDABERGS FF
2013 - UHLSPORT

BK HÄCKEN
2013 - NIKE

DJURGÅRDENS IF
2013 - ADIDAS

DJURGÅRDENS IF
2013 - AWAY - ADIDAS

GAIS
2013 - PUMA

GEFLE IF
2013 - UMBRO

GIF SUNDSVALL
2013 - ADIDAS

HALMSTADS BK
2013 - PUMA

HAMMARBY IF
2013 - KAPPA

HELSINGBORGS IF
2013 - PUMA

IF BROMMAPOJKARNA
2013 - ADIDAS

IF ELFSBORG
2013 - UMBRO

IFK GÖTEBORG
2013 - ADIDAS

IFK NORRKÖPING
2013 - PUMA

KALMAR FF
2013 - PUMA

MALMÖ FF
2013 - PUMA

MJÄLLBY AIF
2013 - UMBRO

ÖREBRO SK
2013 - PUMA

ÖSTERS IF
2013 - PUMA

SYRIANSKA FC
2013 - NIKE

Finland

NATIONAL TEAM
2013 - ADIDAS

NATIONAL TEAM
2013 - AWAY - ADIDAS

FC HONKA
2013 - UMBRO

FC LAHTI
2013 - JOMA

FF JARO
2013 - ERREA

HJK
2013 - ADIDAS

HJK
2013 - AWAY - ADIDAS

IFK MARIEHAMN
2013 - PUMA

INTER TURKU
2013 - NIKE

JJK
2013 - NIKE

KUPS
2013 - PUMA

MYPA
2013 - PUMA

ROPS
2013 - ADIDAS

TPS
2013 - PUMA

VPS
2013 - NIKE

(Europe continued)

AUSTRIA
2013 - PUMA

BOSNIA-HERZEGOVINA
2013 - AWAY - LEGEA

BULGARIA
2013 - KAPPA

HUNGARY
2013 - ADIDAS

KAZAKHSTAN
2013 - ADIDAS

MALTA
2013 - GIVOVA

MONTENEGRO
2013 - LEGEA

NORTHERN IRELAND
2013 - ADIDAS

POLAND
2013 - NIKE

REPUBLIC OF IRELAND
2013 - UMBRO

SCOTLAND
2013 - ADIDAS

SERBIA
2013 - NIKE

SLOVAKIA
2013 - PUMA

SLOVENIA
2013 - AWAY - NIKE

WALES
2013 - AWAY - UMBRO

Brazil

NATIONAL TEAM
2014 - NIKE

NATIONAL TEAM
2013 - AWAY - NIKE

ATLÉTICO MINEIRO
2013 - LUPO SPORT

ATLÉTICO PARANAENSE
2013 - UMBRO

BOTAFOGO
2013 - PUMA

CORINTHIANS
2013 - NIKE

CORINTHIANS
2013 - AWAY - NIKE

CORITIBA
2013 - NIKE

CRICIÚMA
2013 - KANXA

CRUZEIRO
2013 - OLYMPIKUS

CRUZEIRO
2013 - AWAY - OLYMPIKUS

ESPORTE CLUBE BAHIA
2012 - NIKE

ESPORTE CLUBE BAHIA
2012 - AWAY - NIKE

FLAMENGO
2013 - ADIDAS

FLAMENGO
2013 - AWAY - ADIDAS

FLUMINENSE
2013 - ADIDAS

FLUMINENSE
2013 - AWAY - ADIDAS

GOIÁS
2013 - PUMA

GOIÁS
2013 - AWAY - PUMA

GRÊMIO
2013 - TOPPER

GRÊMIO
2013 - AWAY - TOPPER

INTERNACIONAL
2013 - NIKE

NÁUTICO
2013 - PENALTY

NÁUTICO
2013 - AWAY - PENALTY

PONTE PRETA
2013 - PULSE

PORTUGUESA
2013 - LUPO SPORT

PORTUGUESA
2013 – AWAY - LUPO SPORT

SANTOS
2013 - NIKE

SÃO PAULO
2013 - PENALTY

SÃO PAULO
2013 - AWAY - PENALTY

VASCO DA GAMA
2013 - PENALTY

VITÓRIA
2013 - PENALTY

VITÓRIA
2013 - AWAY - PENALTY

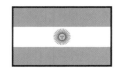

Argentina

NATIONAL TEAM
2014 - ADIDAS

NATIONAL TEAM
2012 - AWAY - ADIDAS

ALL BOYS
2012 - THIRD - BALONPIE

ARGENTINOS JUNIORS
2012 - AWAY - OLYMPIKUS

ARSENAL
2012 - LOTTO

ARSENAL
2012 - THIRD - LOTTO

ATLÉTICO RAFAELA
2012 - AWAY - AR

ATLÉTICO BELGRANO
2012 - THIRD - LOTTO

BOCA JUNIORS
2012 - NIKE

BOCA JUNIORS
2012 - AWAY - NIKE

COLÓN (SANTA FE)
2012 - UMBRO

COLÓN (SANTA FE)
2012 - AWAY - UMBRO

ESTUDIANTES (LA PLATA)
2012 - AWAY - ADIDAS

GODOY CRUZ
2012 - AWAY - LOTTO

INDEPENDIENTE
2012 - PUMA

LANÚS
2012 - OLYMPIKUS

NEWELL'S OLD BOYS
2012 - AWAY - TOPPER

QUILMES
2012 - THIRD - LOTTO

RACING CLUB
2012 - AWAY - OLYMPIKUS

RACING CLUB
2012 - THIRD - OLYMPIKUS

RIVER PLATE
2012 - ADIDAS

RIVER PLATE
2012 - AWAY - ADIDAS

RIVER PLATE
2012 - THIRD - ADIDAS

SAN LORENZO
2012 - AWAY - LOTTO

SAN LORENZO
2012 - THIRD - LOTTO

SAN MARTÍN (SAN JUAN)
2012 - MITRE

SAN MARTÍN (SAN JUAN)
2012 - AWAY - MITRE

SAN MARTÍN (SAN JUAN)
2012 - THIRD - MITRE

TIGRE
2012 - KAPPA

UNIÓN (SANTA FE)
2012 - TBS

UNIÓN (SANTA FE)
2012 - AWAY - TBS

VÉLEZ SARSFIELD
2012 - TOPPER

VÉLEZ SARSFIELD
2012 - THIRD - TOPPER

Chile

NATIONAL TEAM
2014 – PUMA

ANTOFAGASTA
2012 – TRAINING

COBRESAL
2012 – LOTTO

HUACHIPATO
2012 – MITRE

PALESTINO
2012 – TRAINING

**CD UNIVERSIDAD
DE CONCEPCIÓN**
2012 – PENALTY

Ecuador

NATIONAL TEAM
2013 - MARATHON

BARCELONA
2013 - MARATHON

DEPORTIVO QUITO
2013 - FILA

EL NACIONAL
2013 - LOTTO

EMELEC
2013 - WARRIOR

LDU DE QUITO
2013 - UMBRO

Mexico

NATIONAL TEAM
2014 - ADIDAS

NATIONAL TEAM
2013 - AWAY - ADIDAS

ATLANTE
2013 - KAPPA

ATLANTE
2013 - AWAY - KAPPA

ATLANTE
2013 - THIRD - KAPPA

ATLAS
2013 - NIKE

ATLAS
2013 – AWAY – NIKE

CD LÉON
2013 – PIRMA

CD LÉON
2013 – THIRD – PIRMA

CF AMÉRICA
2013 – NIKE

CF AMÉRICA
2013 – AWAY – NIKE

CF AMÉRICA
2013 – THIRD – NIKE

CF PACHUCA
2013 – NIKE

CF PACHUCA
2013 – AWAY – NIKE

CLUB TIJUANA
2013 – NIKE

CRUZ AZUL
2013 - UMBRO

GUADALAJARA
2013 - ADIDAS

JAGUARES DE CHIAPAS
2013 - JOMA

JAGUARES DE CHIAPAS
2013 - AWAY - JOMA

MONARCAS
2013 - NIKE

MONTERREY
2013 - NIKE

MONTERREY
2013 - AWAY - NIKE

MONTERREY
2013 - THIRD - NIKE

PUEBLA
2013 - PIRMA

PUMAS UNAM
2013 - PUMA

QUERÉTARO
2013 - PIRMA

SAN LUIS
2013 - PIRMA

SANTOS LAGUNA
2013 - PUMA

SANTOS LAGUNA
2013 - AWAY - PUMA

TIGRES
2013 - ADIDAS

TIGRES
2013 - AWAY - ADIDAS

TOLUCA
2013 - UNDER ARMOUR

TOLUCA
2013 - THIRD - UNDER ARMOUR

Colombia

NATIONAL TEAM
2014 - ADIDAS

CHICÓ FC
2012 - WALON

CÚCUTA
2012 - FSS

CÚCUTA
2012 - AWAY - FSS

ENVIGADO
2012

JUNIOR
2012 - AWAY - PUMA

LA EQUIDAD
2012

MILLONARIOS
2012 - AWAY - ADIDAS

PASTO
2012 - AWAY - KEUKA

PATRIOTAS
2012 - FSS

REAL CARTAGENA
2012 - LOTTO

REAL CARTAGENA
2012 - THIRD - LOTTO

ITAGÜÍ
2012 - FSS

ITAGÜÍ
2012 - THIRD - FSS

TOLIMA
2012 - MITRE

Uruguay

NATIONAL TEAM
2014 - PUMA

BELLA VISTA
2012 - MGR SPORT

CENTRAL ESPAÑOL
2012 - MATGEOR

CERRO LARGO
2012 - AWAY - MASS

DANUBIO
2012 - MASS

DEFENSOR
2012 - PENALTY

EL TANQUE SISLEY
2012 - MGR SPORT

FÉNIX
2012 - AWAY - MGR SPORT

JUVENTUD
2012 - MENPI

LIVERPOOL
2012 - MGR SPORT

MONTEVIDEO WANDERERS
2012 - MGR SPORT

NACIONAL
2012 - UMBRO

PEÑAROL
2012 - THIRD - PUMA

PROGRESO
2012 - MATGEOR

RACING CM
2012 - AWAY - MASS

United States

NATIONAL TEAM
2013 - NIKE

NATIONAL TEAM
2013 - AWAY - NIKE

CHICAGO FIRE
2013 - ADIDAS

CHICAGO FIRE
2013 - AWAY - ADIDAS

CHIVAS USA
2013 - ADIDAS

COLORADO RAPIDS
2013 - ADIDAS

COLORADO RAPIDS
2013 - AWAY - ADIDAS

COLUMBUS CREW
2013 - ADIDAS

COLUMBUS CREW
2013 - AWAY - ADIDAS

DC UNITED
2013 - ADIDAS

DC UNITED
2013 - AWAY - ADIDAS

FC DALLAS
2013 - ADIDAS

FC DALLAS
2013 - AWAY - ADIDAS

HOUSTON DYNAMO
2013 - ADIDAS

LA GALAXY
2013 - ADIDAS

LA GALAXY
2013 - AWAY - ADIDAS

NEW ENGLAND REVOLUTION
2013 - ADIDAS

NEW YORK RED BULLS
2013 - ADIDAS

PHILADELPHIA UNION
2013 - ADIDAS

PORTLAND TIMBERS
2013 - ADIDAS

REAL SALT LAKE
2013 - ADIDAS

SAN JOSE EARTHQUAKES
2013 - ADIDAS

SEATTLE SOUNDERS
2013 - ADIDAS

SPORTING KANSAS CITY
2013 - ADIDAS

Canada

NATIONAL TEAM
2013 - UMBRO

MONTREAL IMPACT
2013 - ADIDAS

MONTREAL IMPACT
2013 - THIRD - ADIDAS

TORONTO FC
2013 - ADIDAS

TORONTO FC
2013 - AWAY - ADIDAS

VANCOUVER WHITECAPS
2013 - ADIDAS

ANTIGUA AND BARBUDA
2013 - PEAK

BELIZE
2013 - AWAY - KEUKA

BERMUDA
2013 - SCORE

BOLIVIA
2013 - WALON

COSTA RICA
2013 - LOTTO

CUBA
2013 - ADIDAS

EL SALVADOR
2013 – MITRE

GUATEMALA
2013 – UMBRO

HONDURAS
2013 – JOMA

JAMAICA
2013 – KAPPA

PANAMA
2013 – LOTTO

PARAGUAY
2013 – ADIDAS

PERU
2013 – UMBRO

TRINIDAD AND TOBAGO
2013 – ADIDAS

VENEZUELA
2013 – ADIDAS

Tunisia

NATIONAL TEAM
2013 - BURRDA SPORT

CA BIZERTIN
2013 - UHLSPORT

CLUB AFRICAIN
2013 - LEGEA

CS SFAXIEN
2013 - NIKE

ESPÉRANCE SPORTIVE DE TUNIS
2013 - NIKE

ÉTOILE SPORTIVE DU SAHEL
2013 - MACRON

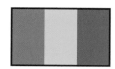

Mali

NATIONAL TEAM
2013 - AIRNESS

AS RÉAL
2013

DJOLIBA
2013

ONZE CRÉATEURS
2013 - LEGEA

STADE MALIEN
2013

USFAS
2013

Morocco

NATIONAL TEAM
2013 - ADIDAS

CR AL HOCEIMA
2013

FAR RABAT
2013 - UHLSPORT

RAJA CASABLANCA
2013 - LOTTO

RENAISSANCE DE BERKANE
2013 - ADIDAS

WYDAD CASABLANCA
2013

Algeria

NATIONAL TEAM
2013 - PUMA

CR BÉLOUIZDAD
2013 - JOMA

CS CONSTANTINE
2013 - KCS

ES SÉTIF
2013 - JOMA

JS KABYLIE
2013 - ADIDAS

MC ALGER
2013 - JOMA

Ivory Coast

NATIONAL TEAM
2014 - PUMA

AFRICA SPORTS
2013

ASEC MIMOSAS
2013

ASI D'ABENGOUROU
2013

CO KORHOGO
2013 - MADSPORT

DENGUÉLÉ SPORT
2013 - PUMA

DJÉKANOU
2013 - PUMA

EFYM
2013 - ADIDAS

ES BINGERVILLE
2013

JCA
2013 - PUMA

SC GAGNOA
2013

SÉWÉ SPORT
2013 - MASS

SOA
2013

STELLA D´ADJAMÉ
2013 - UHLSPORT

USC BASSAM
2013 - ADIDAS

South Africa

NATIONAL TEAM
2013 - PUMA

NATIONAL TEAM
2013 - AWAY - PUMA

AJAX CAPE TOWN
2013 - ADIDAS

AMAZULU
2013 - AWAY - ADIDAS

BLACK LEOPARDS
2013 - AWAY - KAPPA

BLOEMFONTEIN CELTIC
2013 - REEBOK

BLOEMFONTEIN CELTIC
2013 - AWAY - REEBOK

FREE STATE STARS
2013 - AWAY - MAXED

KAIZER CHIEFS
2013 - NIKE

KAIZER CHIEFS
2013 - THIRD - NIKE

MAMELODI SUNDOWNS
2013 - AWAY - NIKE

MOROKA SWALLOWS
2013 - AWAY - PUMA

ORLANDO PIRATES
2013 - ADIDAS

PLATINUM STARS
2013 - UMBRO

PRETORIA UNIVERSITY
2013 - AWAY - UMBRO

Egypt

NATIONAL TEAM
2013 - ADIDAS

AL AHLY CAIRO
2013 - ADIDAS

AL ITTIHAD
2013 - DIADORA

ARAB CONTRACTORS
2013 - UMBRO

PETROJET
2013 - UMBRO

ZAMALEK
2013 - ADIDAS

ANGOLA
2013 – ADIDAS

BENIN
2013 – AIRNESS

BOTSWANA
2013 – UMBRO

BURKINA FASO
2013 – PUMA

CAMEROON
2013 – PUMA

CAPE VERDE
2013 – TEPA

CONGO
2013 - UHLSPORT

CONGO DR
2013 - ERREÀ

ETHIOPIA
2013 - ADIDAS

GABON
2013 - PUMA

GHANA
2013 - PUMA

GUINEA
2013 - AIRNESS

KENYA
2013 - KELME

LESOTHO
2013 - BASUTOLAND INK

MALAWI
2013 - PUMA

MOZAMBIQUE
2013 - LOCATONI

NAMIBIA
2013 - PUMA

NIGER
2013 - TOVIO

NIGERIA
2013 - ADIDAS

RWANDA
2013 - ADIDAS

SENEGAL
2013 - PUMA

TANZANIA
2013 - UHLSPORT

TOGO
2013 - PUMA

ZAMBIA
2013 - NIKE

South Korea

NATIONAL TEAM
2014 - NIKE

NATIONAL TEAM
2013 - AWAY - NIKE

BUSAN I´PARK
2013 - PUMA

CHUNNAM DRAGONS
2013 - KELME

DAEJEON CITIZEN
2013 - KAPPA

FC SEOUL
2013 - LE COQ SPORTIF

GANGWON FC
2013 - ASTORE

GYEONGNAM FC
2013 - AWAY - HUMMEL

INCHEON UNITED
2013 - LE COQ SPORTIF

JEJU UNITED
2013 - AWAY - KIKA

JEONBUK HYUNDAI MOTORS FC
2013 - HUMMEL

POHANG STEELERS
2013 - ATEMI

SEONGNAM ILHWA CHUNMA
2013 - UHLSPORT

SUWON SAMSUNG BLUEWINGS
2013 - ADIDAS

ULSAN HYUNDAI HORANGI
2013 - DIADORA

japan

NATIONAL TEAM
2014 – ADIDAS

NATIONAL TEAM
2013 – AWAY – ADIDAS

ALBIREX NIIGATA
2013 – ADIDAS

ALBIREX NIIGATA
2013 – AWAY – ADIDAS

CEREZO OSAKA
2013 – MIZUNO

CEREZO OSAKA
2013 – AWAY – MIZUNO

FC TOKYO
2013 - ADIDAS

FC TOKYO
2013 - AWAY - ADIDAS

JÚBILO IWATA
2013 - PUMA

JÚBILO IWATA
2013 - AWAY - PUMA

KASHIMA ANTLERS
2013 - NIKE

KASHIMA ANTLERS
2013 - AWAY - NIKE

KASHIWA REYSOL
2013 - YONEX

KAWASAKI FRONTALE
2013 - PUMA

KAWASAKI FRONTALE
2013 - AWAY - PUMA

NAGOYA GRAMPUS EIGHT
2013 - LE COQ SPORTIF

NAGOYA GRAMPUS EIGHT
2013 - AWAY - LE COQ SPORTIF

OITA TRINITA
2013 - PUMA

OMIYA ARDIJA
2013 - UNDER ARMOUR

SAGAN TOSU
2013 - WARRIOR

SAGAN TOSU
2013 - AWAY - WARRIOR

SANFRECCE HIROSHIMA
2013 - NIKE

SANFRECCE HIROSHIMA
2013 - AWAY - NIKE

SHIMIZU S-PULSE
2013 - PUMA

SHIMIZU S-PULSE
2013 - AWAY - PUMA

SHONAN BELLMARE
2013 - PENALTY

URAWA RED DIAMONDS
2013 - NIKE

URAWA RED DIAMONDS
2013 - THIRD - NIKE

VEGALTA SENDAI
2013 - OASICS

VENTFORET KOFU
2013 - MIZUNO

VENTFORET KOFU
2013 - AWAY - MIZUNO

YOKOHAMA F MARINOS
2013 - ADIDAS

YOKOHAMA F MARINOS
2013 - AWAY - ADIDAS

Australia

NATIONAL TEAM
2013 - NIKE

BRISBANE ROAR
2013 - PUMA

CENTRAL COAST MARINERS
2013 - KAPPA

MELBOURNE VICTORY
2013 - AWAY - ADIDAS

PERTH GLORY
2013 - BLADES

SYDNEY FC
2013 - ADIDAS

Uzbekistan

NATIONAL TEAM
2013 - JOMA

MASH'AL MUBAREK
2013 - ADIDAS

NAVBAHOR NAMANGAN
2013 - ADIDAS

NEFTCHI FERGANA
2013 - ADIDAS

PAKHTAKOR TASHKENT
2013 - ADIDAS

PAKHTAKOR TASHKENT
2013 - THIRD - ADIDAS

China PR

NATIONAL TEAM
2013 - ADIDAS

BEIJING GUO'AN
2013 - NIKE

CHANGCHUN YATAI
2013 - NIKE

DALIAN AERBIN
2013 - NIKE

GUANGZHOU EVERGRANDE
2013 - NIKE

GUANGZHOU R&F
2013 - NIKE

GUIZHOU RENHE
2013 - NIKE

HANGZHOU GREENTOWN
2013 - NIKE

JIANGSU SAINTY
2013 - NIKE

QINGDAO JONOON
2013 - NIKE

SHANDONG LUNENG
2013 - NIKE

SHANGHAI SHENHUA
2013 - NIKE

SHANGHAI SIPG
2013 - NIKE

TIANJIN TEDA
2013 - NIKE

WUHAN ZALL
2013 - NIKE

Malaysia

NATIONAL TEAM
2013 - NIKE

NATIONAL TEAM
2013 - AWAY - NIKE

DARUL TAKZIM FC
2013 - THIRD - KAPPA

KELANTAN
2013 - WARRIORS

PAHANG
2013 - STOBI

SELANGOR
2013 - KAPPA

Qatar

NATIONAL TEAM
2013 - NIKE

AL GHARAFA
2013 - ERREA

AL SADD
2013 - BURRDA SPORT

AL WAKRAH
2013 - NIKE

LEKHWIYA
2013 - BURRDA SPORT

QATAR SC
2013 - ADIDAS

BRUNEI DARUSSALAM
2013 - LOTTO

HONG KONG
2013 - NIKE

INDIA
2013 - NIKE

INDONESIA
2013 - NIKE

IRAQ
2013 - AWAY - PEAK

LAOS
2013 - THIRD - FBT

MACAU
2013 - UCAN

NEW ZEALAND
2013 - NIKE

OMAN
2013 - TAJ

PAKISTAN
2013 - VISION

SINGAPORE
2013 - AWAY - NIKE

TAJIKISTAN
2013 - THIRD - LI-NING

UNITED ARAB EMIRATES
2013 - ERREA

VIETNAM
2013 - AWAY - NIKE

YEMEN
2013 - ADIDAS

Index by club names

Table of contents

Picture credits